With Thanks

Also by the author:

With Hope

With Thanks

Jeanne Hammond

BLAGDON PRESS
BROADSTAIRS

With Thanks

First Published 1993
ISBN 1 897944 21 7

Acknowledgements

I would like to thank Connie for her encouragement in getting *With Thanks* started; Sylvia for sorting and typing for so many hours; Sue for adding the full stops and commas; Ron for so much valuable advice; and Seth for the final touches

Some of the names in this book have been changed. Those whose correct names have been used have given their permission.

Typeset and printed in Great Britain for
BLAGDON PRESS
The Basement, 19 Victoria Parade, BROADSTAIRS, Kent
CT10 1QL by
Blagdon Information Systems, Broadstairs, Kent

Before We Begin

Jeanne Hammond was born on a bleak day in December 1933 at St Thomas's Hospital, London. Small, with a mop of bright red hair and a hunger that was not satisfied during the first year.

Many childhood traumas followed, the most impressive was the day that World War II began.

Between the bombing and ill health, Jeanne's schooling suffered considerably, but her mother was young at heart, had a good imagination and was clever with her hands. Jeanne inherited these qualities and enjoyed the love she received.

Jeanne became a Christian when she was fourteen years old.

FORWARD

I have enjoyed writing this book which has taken me about three years, done mostly during my holidays in France, with the re-writing squeezed in between other duties.

It started as a life story and has ended with the story of my family. That is not surprising as my work has never been a job but a way of life. Some of my memories have been hard to commit to paper, others impossible. There will be readers who may be disappointed that their names are not mentioned, no slight is intended. To have included all the adults and children who have passed my way would have been an impossible task.

Many young people have lived and worked with me, from all of them I have learned a great deal. Many of them have become my friends and fellowship with them has been sweet. There have been a few for whom I was just an employer. That, I feel, has been a pity because the ingredient of joy has been missed.

Perhaps one day I will have time to write another book. If the next years of my life are as full as those that have passed, I shall not lack material.

I hope that, in my writing, I have been able to capture enough of the joys and pain to make interesting reading. Perhaps something in these pages will help you in your life, or help you to understand our friends with a mental handicap a little better.

I can only thank the Lord Jesus for allowing me to meet so many interesting people.

JEANNE HAMMOND, April 1993

Prologue

"Good morning Miss Hardcourt, you sent for me?"

"Yes Jeanne. I hear that you must leave school at the end of this term."

"Yes Miss Hardcourt."

"I know that you have to help your mother over the summer, but what do you want to do with your life?"

"Oh! I'm going to be nanny miss. I'm writing to Dr Barnado's. I want to train at Babies Castle, in Hawkhurst, miss."

"My dear; you must forget about that. With your school record and your physical disability, no training school will accept you. Perhaps you can find a washing-up post near to your home. I hope your mother will be better soon."

"Yes miss. Thank you miss."

I left the room with my mind in a whirl. Here I was aged fourteen years and only fit to wash up. All my childhood I had only wanted to look after babies. With those dreams smashed, what would become of me? I didn't like washing up.

I would show her. I would write to Dr Barnardo's. I would be a nanny

CHAPTER 1
BABIES CASTLE

What a Christmas present! What excitement! What a panic! I was actually on my way towards my impossible dream! I was sixteen and ready to start my training at Babies Castle, a Dr Barnado's home in Kent. It was a large, rambling house full of babies and children, plus a group of young teenagers all seeking to become Nursery Nurses. Five new students started their training on that day in January; one left within a few days. After three months two others, the twins, were re-employed as domestic staff. The remaining girl and I became special friends. She grew ill and had to leave after eight or nine months, later she died of leukaemia.

The work, over the next three years, was hard and long, no forty-hour week or eight-hour day, but I remember those years as having been fun and have never ceased to be grateful to those in charge of my training.

The first year was concerned mainly with housework, laundry, some kitchen work, learning to obey orders, and preparing trays for sick children to be served for

"Matron's Tea". Oh! those thinly cut sandwiches were such a problem, no ready sliced bread in those days!

As I was the only student left in my group, I was obliged to take my lectures with both the group above and the group below me. The uniform of first year students was pink dresses, everyone looked very smart but with my bright red hair I never looked my best. In September there was an Open Day, Matron met me in the corridor the day before and sent me to the seamstress to get a green dress, the colour for the second year. She met me afterwards and said, "How nice you look," - that was Matron! She was hard when it came to training, showing us the dust we had left behind by wiping her white handkerchief along the offending article. She inspected our work every day, but she was kindness itself. The first winter was very cold yet all the nappies and sheets had to be hung outside on clotheslines, no matter the weather, "to kill germs" we were told, then brought in frozen stiff after two or three hours. The hanging out and gathering in could take up to two hours each way, becoming slower as fingers got colder. Occasionally we were spurred on when Matron and the cook took pity on us and came to help. When our stint in the laundry came in the summer, it was a joy to be outside.

During the first year it was a privilege to be able to take the little ones out in their prams, usually two to each pram. These large, stately carriages were old but highly polished and shining. We each did a few weeks in the kitchen. Our life there was punctuated by the cook lustily bursting forth into song, mostly good old hymns in fact she could be heard quite a distance from the kitchen. We all loved to join in, I wonder if she realized how much we enjoyed her singing?

My second year of training was spent working in the nurseries. I have vivid memories of my first days with the babies: shaking so much that the poor baby cried; being so frightened of getting it all wrong, learning the two ways of sterilizing. Yes, the cold method was slowly taking the place of boiling the equipment. I mastered the art of calculating feeds, in spite of my poor maths, but I cannot remember how long it took me.

Babies were always washed and dressed on the lap. All the nappies had to be folded just so; no disposable nappies for us! How difficult it all was when we were too nervous to let go of the kicking baby; and the terrible moment when our slippery, soapy baby had to be lifted into the bath. A brief moment of panic then it was done; the relief that it was over for today and the promise to do better tomorrow; the thought that if my baby would not take his feed or cried too much while I changed him, would they think that I was no good at the job?

With each day my confidence grew and very soon I was not the newest student; someone else, just as nervous, had taken my place.

One morning, when all the babies had been fed and the staff had gone to breakfast, I was left to clear up and to change two or three babies. They were sitting in their chairs, fortunately low-chairs, when one child slid down onto the floor. She was not hurt but her head was stuck between the seat and the tray. Whatever I tried, I could not get her out. She could not go down and there was not enough room to pull her up. When help came, the tray had to be sawn off before she could be freed. When the sister-in-charge of the babies had first seen these chairs, she had predicted that something like this would happen, but why did it happen to me?

The "tweenies", at that messy age of nine to eighteen months, were fun but hard work, with always one mess or another to clear up. Little characters, all determined to have their own way and to do things by themselves - if that was not allowed, they would not do it at all: Don't you all know how it is? While dealing with a minor crisis on one side of the nursery, Johnnie would be eating as much of his neighbours food as he could, while Jane would be peering out from under her up-turned bowl with custard running down her cheeks.

They all looked so lovely when they were clean at last and nicely tucked up in bed; although there was usually one not tired and trying to climb the curtains. Each one in turn taking the first steps and saying the first words; news of which quickly spread among the students, who, when they passed, popped in to applaud.

My free time was always very full. First and foremost the lecture notes had to be written up. I was no scholar so it took a long time and alas, was not well presented. What a blessing to have a Matron and Sister Tutor who were so patient, followed by a second Sister equally patient. This sister helped me a lot with my written work by encouraging me to complete short essays within a given time. This helped me to write more quickly.

Cycling was one of my hobbies and, on a day off, I often rode from Hawkhurst to Bodiam Castle, then on to Rye and Winchelsea and the coastal road to Hastings. There I would take a dip in the sea before cycling back to Hawkhurst in the early evening. I still enjoy picnics in the open air.

One evening each week we were obliged to do "Physical Exercise" or dancing, it varied from time to time and was arranged by Matron. In the summer we had a coach to take us swimming in the sea at Hastings. As I look back, I wonder how we found the energy for such strenuous activity after our hard day's work.

We had two weeks' holiday each year. Mine were usually spent Youth Hostelling with a friend. Once we went round the Isle of Wight. Another was a very memorable 155 mile trip to and around the Cotswolds, passing through Oxford, going as far north as Stratford-on-Avon and as far south as Bath. We stayed in different places every night, from small thatched-roofed cottages to large Youth hostels. We came back via Arundel.

My home was still in Folkestone and I went there about once a month. I like to think that I helped Mum with her Guest House, but I rather doubt it.

When I was at home I continued going to my original Church, but during my training days I felt no need to join a church, partly because it was so far away and also because we had prayer times with Matron who was a retired Missionary.

The upper age group, from two-and-a-half to five years, was divided between three nurseries. Students also had to spend some time in the Nursery School where the older children went. These children were learning to do things for themselves, to share and help. They had plenty of advice to give on how things should be done, especially if you were a novice in their midst. The youngsters were well aware of the difference between the first and second year students.

It was during my time with one of these groups that I was able to take the twins, Sue and Roger, home with me for a holiday. They were four years old and had no memories other than Babies Castle. They called my parents "Mum and Dad" right from the start, it seemed very natural. Everything was so new and exciting for them. When my father removed his false teeth, they spent a long time trying to take out their own and each other's. They were surprised that we bathed, washed our hair and cleaned our teeth; their lives in the nursery and the students' private lives did not overlap. These two children were adopted and I was gratified that they had an opportunity to see life in an ordinary family, albeit only for a short time.

I remember the walks and the picnics in the log field; the influx of the hop pickers, with the heavy scent of the hops drying in the evenings. Getting four or five children ready to go out in the winter seemed to take forever, with all those winter clothes. You could be sure that just as the last mitten was put on, the first "wellie" would be off.

Also recalled are the changes of season with piles of children's clothes waiting to be marked with each child's name. Then there was Christmas Eve and the hurry to tumble excited children into bed so that we could rush away to fill their stockings from the pile of things so kindly donated. We were as excited as the children; "I wonder if Andy would like this?", "Do you think that Debbie would like that?", or "Don't forget Edward, he wants a big comb." Edward had tight black curls, quite uncombable, but his great desire was for a BIG comb!

I had to re-sit my first semi-final examination as I did not answer enough questions. With my improved writing speed I was quicker the second time. The final three months were spent at Barkingside Village Homes, where it was all theory. The house was large with the lower part devoted to lecture rooms and the usual amenity rooms. The students slept upstairs but there was one bed short, so I had to sleep in the village in a room in another house used for senior staff.

These three months were very lonely for me as after supper I was obliged to return alone to my own room. I was supposed to study but seldom did. In the room was a gas fire with a slot meter for two shilling pieces, as I earned only ten shillings a week I could not burn the fire for very long. During this time it snowed and for a long period there was a "pea-soup" smog. If we put any washing out to dry, it was dirtier when we brought it in than before we had washed it. I caught a bad cold and was admitted to hospital with suspected measles, at least it was warm there. I was released from hospital and sent back to my room to recover. Someone from the other house came to visit me and showed me a sitting room in the basement where I could put on the fire without having to feed the meter.

We were certainly well fed and had lots of puddings. I put on weight and for the first time in my life was almost fat.

Final exams were taken and it was time to move on; away from Babies Castle, friends and things familiar. There were good-byes to the many children we had seen grow from tiny babies. We each stepped forth, taking our own route, not knowing what lay ahead. I saw a special friend about three years later; she was then married and we no longer had anything in common so we drifted apart.

On several occasions during these three years I had seen a doctor about the curvature of my spine and the problem with my left arm, which did not function correctly. He thought it could be due to the operation on the TB gland, but did not propose any treatment.

Chapter 2
Jobs

During the next four years I worked as a Nanny for a family in Wimbledon, looking after two little girls and later twins. There was plenty to do but I was happy, learning all the time. The way of life was so different from my home life and the time at Babies Castle. Each summer the family spent a month in Cornwall, at Constantine Bay. I suppose the cottage there must have been quite large but with six in the family plus cook and myself, it always seemed small. The weather was kind, it never rained all day there and even the showers seemed warm. At low tide, pools were left in the sand which were warm and deep enough for the children and I to swim in.

The older child was very timid and I spent a long time trying to encourage her to do things. She was three years old and still going downstairs on her bottom. I did not think she was a slow child, just lacking courage. Slowly she gained confidence and improved, especially when she started dancing classes and Nursery School.

Her sister was a precocious child and liked to show how clever she was. Many times I picked up the younger child to prevent her from doing something before her elder sister.

During my years in Wimbledon I visited a Mother and Baby Home in Putney, which was run by the last Sister Tutor and the Cook from Babies Castle. Sometimes I went on my day off other times in the evening to allow them an evening off. Most of the unmarried mothers there were very young. They went to the home six weeks before their babies were born and stayed until six weeks after. A few babies were taken home but most were adopted, simply because there was no other answer.

God laid on my heart that I was to open a Home to take the babies of these young girls, so that they would have more time and perhaps would find another solution. What He did not tell me was how or when this would happen. I had no money and, with a living-in job, earned very little.

I did not attend a church and had no friends of my own age. Apart from my day off, I did not have much free time. The evening meal was taken late and even if I had something to do, it would have been too late and I was too tired.

During this time I was able to visit my Auntie Eva and her family who lived near Harrow. I spent many happy times there, it was like a second home to me. Sometimes we would meet in Oxford Street to look at the shops; I do not remember us buying much but we had some good days together. I received much help from my Aunt over a period of about ten years. I convalesced with her after two operations and it was in her brother-in-law's house that I first became a foster mother in 1964.

In my fourth year at Wimbledon I became restless, perhaps I was tired, looking after four children is tiring; perhaps I was suffering from a late adolescence, anyway, it was time to move on.

Next I worked for an American family as a temporary Mother's Help, during the birth of a third child. I found the differences in routine and food intriguing, every meal finishing with either a piece of apple or celery. In this family the children received gentle discipline and were not spoilt, as I had been lead to believe in the past. I lived with my aunt and uncle and went to work daily until the mother went into hospital, when I lived-in for about ten days. The days were enjoyable and my two small charges remained happy enough; the evenings proved to be more difficult! The children's father wanted to get too close. In any other situation I would have left but as I had undertaken this job for only six weeks, I thought I could last out. After the children had gone to bed I would do the ironing, barricading the kitchen door with the ironing board. I do not know how fierce I looked brandishing the iron, but he got the message and left me alone. I think I did more ironing in those ten days than I had for several months previously. The mother returned from hospital and I went back to working days only, so the problem was resolved and the remaining weeks passed very quickly.

About this time I had an appointment to see a specialist in one of the London hospitals. An operation on my back was proposed. This particular operation had been performed once before so only offered a fifty per cent chance of success. I was gradually losing the movement in my arm so I agreed, but had to wait some months before it could be done.

On searching through the newspapers I found an interesting advertisement for a Nanny, with qualifications and experience, to work in Geneva, Switzerland. I applied and was interviewed in England where the family was on holiday. I was engaged to look after one little girl aged nine months.

It was arranged that I would meet the father and son at the Port of Dover and travel with them, and their Italian girl who worked in the house, by car to Switzerland. I would be there for about nine months, then I would enter hospital for my operation.

I duly met the car at Dover and we travelled late into the night before stopping at an hotel for some four hours. I found travelling with total strangers difficult. The Italian girl spoke no English and I no Italian, in the darkness we could not even smile at each other.

On arriving at their house, I was shown into an attic room, It did not bother me as I had often slept in an attic, but this one was really dirty with cobwebs and mouse droppings. The room contained an iron bedstead and a dirty wash-basin no curtains, no chair and no-where to put my clothes. Even on my shortest stays away from home, I had been able to unpack. My own family had always been poor but home was clean and comfortable. I had lived away from home for some years and was not prepared for the homesickness which I felt.

The room improved a little with cleaning and my trunk became a dressing table, but it was never a friendly room. Later I discovered that the Italian girl had been moved from this room to a space under the roof with no window and only a mattress with no sheets on the floor. As we could not communicate, I was unable to tell her how sorry I was. I tried to express my anger at her treatment but was told it was none of my business and that her circumstances at home would certainly have been worse. I found that hard to believe but have since realised that it was possibly so. The roof space she had to herself, if she came from a large family she probably never had a place to call her own.

At my interview the family had seemed friendly, but no longer. In my previous employments I had been at least on the fringe of the family. In this house I was a servant, to be told what to do and no discussion. I knew no one in Geneva and did not speak a word of French.

The child's father was British and worked for the United Nations; his wife was Russian. The baby was not allowed to leave the garden, I was not told why. On reflection, it could have been a fear of kidnapping. I will never know. I spent hours walking round and round the tiny garden, talking to my small charge. I sang every nursery rhyme that I knew many times over I felt like a prisoner and was often tempted to leave the garden out of sheer boredom and I was sure that it was not good for the baby to be so shut away.

I found meal times very strange. When the family had eaten, I could sit in the kitchen to have my meal, at a table stacked with dirty crockery. Later I discovered that the Italian girl then had what was left. As we did not eat together, it was several weeks before I realized that the portion left was for her as well, even though there would be only one piece of meat or fish. If I was hungry I hoped that, for both our sakes, the family would not be, or that one of them would not come in for lunch.

About ten days after my arrival in Switzerland, I had a visitor, who called in response to a letter from my home church. This young lady had worked in an hotel in my home town of Folkestone, visiting my church during her stay. I had not met her there as it was while I was working away. I was so pleased to have someone to talk to and I was invited to her home on my next free day. She lived some miles out in the country and how to get there presented a problem. In the garage was a child's cycle which had obviously not been used for some time. I pumped up the tyres and tried it, being small has some advantages and this was one. At the next opportunity I asked about it, and was told that it was an old one once used by the older children, and "Yes" I could use it.

My next day off dawned bright and sunny. After my charge was dressed, breakfasted, her room cleaned, her washing done and hung on the line, I was free to go. I took the cycle and set off. As the cycle was small, I had to peddle fast but soon got used to it. The country was fairly flat so the going was easy and I was free!

What a welcome I received! There was a large family with most of the children still at home; the younger ones going to school and the older ones helping their parents to run an Old People's Home. In a very short time I was accepted as one of the family, free to help with whatever was going on. I spent many very happy days with them and will always be grateful for their loving care. The church was attached to the house and, with difficulty, I managed to be free some Sunday mornings for the service. I would arrive somewhat dishevelled, hot and out of breath, on my small cycle, having ridden as fast as I could, often, I might add, on the wrong side of the road!

At the Old People's Home the washing was done once a month, for the family and the elderly, in a special laundry house in the grounds. Fires were lit under great coppers and the washing would take almost a week with the ironing taking the next two weeks. The quantity of washing to be done brought back memories of my days at Babies Castle.

After six unhappy weeks with the family where I worked, I was thinking of returning home but, as I had not been paid, that was financially impossible. My friends found a new job for me at Pouponiere, a children's nursery on the other side of Geneva and I gave in my notice. The day came for me to leave and I asked for my wages. Eventually, after some trouble, I was paid for one month instead of two. I did not mind too much as I was so pleased to be away from that house. I had made a terrible mistake and was so thankful to be rescued. My friends took me to their home for a few days before I started work at the Pouponiere.

Here I should mention that I could not speak French; it had not been taught at my school. I had been with an English speaking family for two months and I spoke English with my friends. I knew, maybe, thirty to forty French words but nothing more.

Chapter 3
Travels

The Pouponiere had about thirty children of various nationalities, aged from five days to seven years, with about fifteen staff and students of seven nationalities. We spoke a very mixed language with many gesticulations but most of the time we were able to understand each other, we certainly could not argue! I do not know how the children ever managed to speak. Most of the children's parents were away in the mountains having treatment for tuberculosis. The children were often ill; they rarely went out. The house was kept at a constant temperature of between 22° - 25°C day and night. During the winter, the windows were opened only in the mornings for about thirty minutes.

It was interesting work as I moved from group to group, filling in when the students were off duty. The hours were long and the work quite hard. There were eight children in a group with one nurse. The time allowed for bathing was ten minutes for each child, with no time to splash and play, or to learn to dress. The bath-time routine was my most difficult time as I found lifting eight heavy toddlers into a high bath very hard work. Customs and the way of doing things were so different from what I was used to. As there was no one to watch those children not in the bath, they were confined to their beds or to their pots in the bathroom. The pots were placed into holes in a low bench, this stopped them from tipping over and the children from charging about. There was always a race against time to get them fed and tucked up. Staff supper followed and we were not allowed to miss it or to arrive late,

All the toys were kept locked in a very small playroom. This was only occasionally unlocked for the older children, the rest had few things to play with, and, because they had little to do, they played "rough and tumble" and generally pulled each other about.

From the Pouponiere, I visited the countryside around by bus and on foot, often walking on Mt Saleve. One day I took a paddle steamer around Lake Oman, the voyage took all day and was most enjoyable. Bedecked in a large hat and a long sleeved shirt, I thought I was safe from the sun, but my face got badly burnt from the sun's reflection in the water.

From the Pouponiere, it was difficult for me to visit my friends. They lived quite a distance away and, of course,

I no longer had the use of the small cycle. When I was free, I went to a Brethren Church in the old city of Geneva. There I met another large family who took me to their home, just over the border in France. The road to their home went past the end of the road where I worked. They had a farm and their Italian farm workers joined the family for their mid-day meal. There were so many at table that I could arrive without warning, as one more or less made no difference at all.

Again I was allowed to join in whatever activity was taking place when I arrived; picking and preparing fruit for jam or bottling, carrying the afternoon drinks to the workers out in the fields, meeting the children from school. One day I arrived to find half of a cow stretched out on the kitchen table. (Yes, it was an enormous table in a very large kitchen.) This was cut up, weighed, wrapped and labelled for the freezer. It took almost the whole day.

The farm house was built with the animals and farm equipment on the ground floor, opening out into the yard. There was not much machinery, horses were still used for most of the work. The front of the house faced the garden on the opposite side. The family lived upstairs. It was a very long house, divided into three, occupied by the elderly parents and their two married sons.

To arrive at the farm, I caught a bus from the end of the road which took me across the border to the small town of St Julien. From there I walked along a cart track for over two miles. My friends were kind enough to return me to the bus by car in the evening, after supper.

One evening I boarded the bus home and as it drew near to the frontier, I looked for my passport but could not find it anywhere. I had not been asked to show it on the morning journey. It was the last bus and, if I had to get off, I was worried how I would get back to work. It was my first experience of such a situation and I was embarrassed as I tried to explain. Anyway, the bus waited while the Customs man phoned to confirm that I did work at the Pouponiere.

Everyone on the farm had their own job to do. The youngest boy in the family was about three years old, his mother cooked on a wood burning stove and, from time to time, would ring a little bell at the yard door. After a while her young son would climb up the long flight of steps, carrying a few small logs or some kindling in a box. I remember him well, with his glasses large on his head.

One day the Grandparents took me, with one of the grandchildren, on a trip to see Mont Blanc. It was the first time I had been in the high mountains, still white with snow in summer. The flowers had such bright colours, wild rhododendrons were blooming and I saw many of the flowers that we cultivate in gardens at home.

Recently I have visited my friends again and the whole of the countryside in this area has changed. It was difficult to find the farms as a great motorway cuts through the farmland. It all looks so different. Progress they call it!!

In March of my twenty-third year, after eight months in Geneva, I was on my way back home for the proposed operation, but with an offer I could not refuse - to return by mid-July to relieve the Matron for her holiday and to stay another year.

The operation, in the Great Portland Street hospital, consisted of taking a tissue graft from my thigh and stitching it into my back, thus holding the shoulder blade at a better angle. The operation went well and I was soon up and about. The graft took a long time to heal and the whole arm and shoulder had to be immobilised for almost three months.

I spent a month in the hospital and during that time I met some lovely people I grew quite fond of one Christian lady and still have the pleasure of writing to her, over thirty years later. Despite her severe disabilities, she has never stopped working for the Lord. She must be quite elderly now as she was no chicken when I first met her so long ago.

The big day came when all the strapping was removed and I was given a leather back brace to wear. Later this chafed under the arms and proved quite uncomfortable, especially at night. The most immediate task was to get the arm working. The skin at the elbow joint had grown very tight. I turned down a further stay in hospital and, after a chat with the physiotherapist, I went home to start exercising. In three weeks I was discharged from the hospital and a week later was on my way back to Switzerland, to take up where I had left off,

The Matron was away for a month and on her return I was relieved to hand back control to its rightful owner; happy to know that I had coped, even with my limited French, and that the house was intact and all the children well.

After about three months I could not lift my arm, it was no better than before the operation. This was a big disappointment. I was told that nothing could be done for a year and I should stay in Geneva and enjoy the experience. I was used to managing with only one and a half arms so was not unduly embarrassed by it.

Heidi, one of the volunteers in this nursery was a Christian and we became good friends. She was Swiss-German but also spoke French and English well. Heidi and I visited many places together one of these was the United Nations palace. I was suitably impressed, it was all so grand. It was so much more enjoyable to be able to share interests with someone. I also found going into the city much easier, though it took me a long time to get used to the traffic on the other side of the road. The countryside was one thing but the town quite another, and all those trams too!!!

By the time my year was up, I had saved enough money to buy a round-ticket to see more of Switzerland. I planned to stay at Youth hostel and the Swiss Houses for Young Women. I took the train up to Zermatt. The climbers woke me early in the morning as they were setting out. What a sight! The valley was still in darkness but the Matterhorn was in brilliant sunshine with no cap of cloud, apparently that is rare. For the first time I saw a whole field of pink autumn crocuses and wild cyclamen in the forest.

I flew like a bird on a chair-lift to Grindelwald. What an experience! It was like being on top of the world. As if seeing Switzerland was not enough, I spent three interesting days in Venice adopted by a fellow traveller and his daughter. They did not think that I should be travelling alone in Italy and the gentleman thought I would be good company for his daughter. Venice was so different from any other city, so many sights and so far to walk. Fortunately I was able to take photographs and relive the experience later.

As mentioned previously, I was no scholar but during the last 20 months I discovered that I could write long letters. My mother kept these letters and I was able to re-read them during my next stay in hospital and, together with my photographs, they brought back happy memories. Unfortunately my letters were later destroyed.

This holiday finished with a week in Heidi's home near the Rhine-falls at Neuhausen. I could hear the falls from my bedroom. Apparently the water was low in the autumn but there seemed a lot to me. I had never seen anything like it before. Heidi's mother was a foster mother to two young children who had bad experiences and were very difficult.

My time in Switzerland came to an end and I left for home. Heidi came to stay in my home for a few days, before joining a family as an au-pair for a year.

In due course I went back to hospital to have the offending arm dealt with. It was four months before I could work again. About this time I saw my first television programme, in black and white, of course.

Time to start work again, this time for a Jewish family in Golders Green. The little girl was two years old and very easy but the four year old boy was "King in his Castle". If he wished to plaster the walls of the toilet that was all right because Nanny would clear it up. While Mummy was in hospital having the new baby, Nanny solved that problem by getting junior to clean up his own mess - just once! He was an intelligent child and never did it again during my stay, which was not for very long. Again the way of life was different and I learned a lot; I also ate more chicken during that brief stay than I ever had before.

When Heidi had completed her year as an au-pair, we went on holiday together to the Isle of Amrum in the North Sea off the German coast Heidi's family were already there with the children.

The weather was mostly very windy. We spent our days on the beach or walking in the dunes. There was not much of anything on this island except an abundance of fresh air and sand. There was a very tall lighthouse next door and seals bathed on the dunes at low tide. We had arrived on a small ferry and there was no traffic. When the little girl became tired she was transported in a laundry cart or given a piggyback.

We found ourselves to be in a nudist colony, as it was called in those days. As there were not many people on the island it did not bother us, just made changing on the beach a little easier!

At the end of my holiday I said goodbye to my friends and returned home to look for work.

I have met this family only once since that time, visiting their home. They took me on some beautiful outings; to the Black Forest in Germany, to the high mountains of Switzerland, and to stay, for the first time, in a chalet on the Randem mountain.

Most years since then we have corresponded. Mutti has gone to be with her Lord and her grandchildren are growing up. Perhaps the family and I will have the opportunity to meet again one day.

After several nanny-help jobs, seeing families settled with new babies, I needed more permanent place of work. I wrote after a situation in Norfolk as a Nanny to twins, first children in a family. The interview was in London; I was engaged and duly set off by train, complete with bicycle.

The house was in the heart of the country, set in park and farm land. I had not expected such a large house. The only time I had been into a similar one was when sight-seeing as a tourist. This house was quite different. It was simply furnished and, despite its size, very homely. Sometimes I was alone in the main house but never felt afraid. One side of the house bordered the drive, the other looked out over the garden, a meadow and a lake, beyond which was woodland. The nursery was on the drive side of the house, at the end of a corridor farthest away from the kitchen. The problem of distance was quickly solved by having my own cooker on which to cook the babies food. I had been trained not to use tins and jars although, by now, they were readily available.

When I arrived the twins were one month old. They were breast fed and had no problems with eating or sleeping. Their mother was always available at feeding time and to play, neither of the twins ever had a bottle. As they grew, everyone in the house gravitated to the nursery for afternoon tea; in the winter it was the warmest place. In summer we spent as much time as possible in the garden, there were many sheltered places to sit and woodland paths to walk.

My bicycle was well used, the countryside was quite flat although it was inclined to be windy. Norwich was about ten miles away. On my days off I would hide my cycle in the hedge and take the bus. I visited Norwich mainly for the market, where I bought off-cuts of material and wool at bargain prices. Later this extended to cots, prams and other small items of furniture.

Although I was very happy with this family, my vision was to open a home for babies. As yet I had no idea when, how or where. My salary was only about £6 per week, so it was still very much a dream, but it became urgent that I should be working towards the goal that I felt the Lord was leading me to.

During the daytime, while my charges were playing, I made clothes for them but once they were in bed, I made baby clothes, dresses, romper suits with smocking and night-gowns all hand embroidered. I knitted all the patterns I had for matinee jackets over and over again. Time was precious and I did not want to waste a minute. I have always liked living in the country, partly I think, because there is less rushing around and more time for the creative things which I enjoy. During the last six months of my time in Norfolk, I painted cots and nursing chairs, renovated old prams and made the bedding, mostly using things given to me.

I learned to drive and bought an old Ford Prefect for £70. It had leather upholstery and had been well looked after by its previous owner, I cleaned it often as it looked lovely when polished. I sold it two years later for £85. I knew nothing about cars as my family had never owned one, neither had any close friends. This car was fine during the summer, but had to be cranked with a starting handle in the winter or when it was damp. I do not think I ever managed to start it alone, but the men on the farm were very good to me and would even give me a tow with the tractor.

One day I was shocked to see what I thought was smoke rising from the bonnet, as I stopped the car was engulfed. I expected an explosion. The garage man came and towed me away, only to find that the radiator was dry. No one had mentioned that it might need a drink from time to time! This man also showed me how to check the oil and add some more, I did not know about that either! The indicators were the type that stuck out at the sides. They were inclined to get bent in the wind and not return to their sockets, so I would be driving along at the great pace of 25 miles per hour, with both indicators extended.

I lived with the family in Norfolk for four years. When the twins were two years old, another little girl was born, who was also a very good baby.

I went to the local Baptist Church which was in the village about two miles away. There I met some very kind people who invited me to their home, sometimes I spent an afternoon with them. As I was on duty on Sunday, I had to ask for time off to go to Church. When working in Service, free time is not always very clear cut. I was not always free on the same day each week and not at all when the parents were absent. I did not feel free to take the children to visit my friends or to take them to my church, however, I did invite my friends to nursery tea on one or two occasions.

On the whole a nanny's life was rather a lonely one. She was everything to the children when the parents were away, which sometimes could be frequent or for long periods. Then, as soon as the parents returned, she had to have the ability to melt away without being hurt, yet be available at the ring of a bell. She would hear many things and must be careful not to gossip. In the upstairs/downstairs context, she was the one in the middle, and it was almost impossible to have a special friendship within the household.

CHAPTER 4
SELF-EMPLOYED

While visiting my Auntie Eva, I talked about my dream of a home for babies and how I was working towards it. She said that her brother-in-law was living in a large house and, since his mother had died, he did not really need so much room; she suggested that I should write to him. This I did and Mr Baker replied, inviting me to visit his house in Dover. He was interested in the idea and thought that perhaps he could move upstairs, leaving me the two lower floors which consisted of four rooms, a kitchen (the old scullery) and a bathroom, also the garden which for a town house was a good size however he needed time to think about it before making a decision.

Some weeks passed before the answer came, it was YES but not for six months. This proved to be perfect timing as there was to be a fourth child, and it was much easier to get a nanny with the prospect of a new baby.

Now, each time I had a few days off together, I loaded the car and set off for my home in Folkestone, crossing on the Woolwich Ferry. I became quite well known because I always had a pram roped to the tail flap. All this equipment was stored in my bedroom at Folkestone. In the end I could not sleep there any more. My mother must have wondered how much more was coming but she never complained.

On one trip, as I was nearing Charing in Kent, I got a flat tyre. Of course, the spare wheel was under the load. By the time I located it, I looked as if I was setting up camp. The AA man was so good, he helped me tie it all on again, all being a pram, a cot and two kitchen chairs. In the many trips I made that was the only problem, apart from the near heart attacks each time I had to drive onto the ferry.

The car was convenient because I was so far from everywhere, but I was never a happy, confident driver and was more than relieved when the car was sold.

Finally I was packed and ready to leave this family from whom I had received such care and kindness for four happy years. I had learned many valuable things, mostly those that come from being alone and making decisions. Another period of my life in which the Lord was preparing me for the future.

Saying good-bye to my three young charges was not easy and I shed many tears in the days that followed. But they had their new Nanny and my work with them was finished. So too was my security! Was I self-employed or unemployed? I considered myself the former so went off to find out about stamping a National Insurance Card.

To fill in time I cleaned bicycles for a friend for a week or two and earned enough to stamp my card and to eat, in that order. In September the day came when I was to move into the house in Dover, planning permission having been granted.

The friend with the bicycles offered himself and his van for the afternoon. Mum and I went with the first load, leaving Dad to follow later. We arrived about 2 pm to discover that we could not get in as no key had been left, however, we gained entry through a back window but could not unlock the front door. The windows were the sash cord type so everything went in that way except my single bed, which we had to leave propped up against the front door. All this activity caused a great stir amongst the neighbours. All those prams, cots and carry-cots, four or five of each, going into the house of a bachelor! Up and down the road the curtains were moving continuously!

Mum, Dad and I said good-bye to the friend and we looked round to take stock. Everywhere was dark brown or dark green, some rooms were both colours. Now, thinking back, it should have been depressing but I was young and full of enthusiasm for this new adventure. I had been waiting and working for this for about three and a half years.

Mum was in this venture right from the start and her enthusiasm matched mine. She decided to start on the kitchen and ended up scrubbing the walls with a pan scourer.

What I had designated as the kitchen was in fact the scullery, 5 ft square with two doors. The original kitchen was now to be a living room. An Ideal boiler had been installed for the heating. It was a lovely, sunny room and once it was clean and redecorated, it was very comfortable with the linoleum given to me as a gift by my previous employers.

Tea that first night was to be boiled eggs, simple enough with the eggs on serviette rings as we had no egg-cups. We found one teaspoon which we shared and, until the knives came to light some time later, Dad's penknife came in handy. Altogether it was a very strange tea-time.

Mr Baker came home to find my bed still propped against the front door, as we had all arrived via the window. This was the beginning of a twenty-four year friendship. Over the next six months we worked together to improve and brighten the property.

My immediate need was to find employment that would bring in enough to pay the rent, my food and National Insurance Stamps, with as few hours work as possible.

As usual just the right job found me, although it was for only about three months. Cleaning in a boy's residential college from 9 am, until 1.30 pm, for five days each week, with dinner included. I was used to hard work and was not put off by the size of the dining room. The floor polisher was an enormous machine with a very strong will of its own. I would be getting on very nicely when, suddenly, it would rush off to the left or the right with me hanging on behind. Anyone crossing the dining-room when the polisher was in control, did so at their own peril.

What a blessing were those dinners! Being my main meal of the day, they cut my food expenses considerably. Also I did not have to spend time preparing food on my return home at 2 pm. I would sleep or read for an hour then carry on with the decorating. With a short break for tea at about 5.30 pm, I worked until 8.30 pm then fell into bed. No sleeping problems for me!

Following on from the College I went to do housework for Joan, a friend from church. She had elderly parents and they had just had some building work done. This gave me the required amount of money for my immediate living expenses. Joan continued to be a very supportive friend throughout my years in Dover.

For those six months my days were much the same. Getting up at 6 am, painting and decorating until 8 am, then breakfast and off to work for 9 am. Once again the bicycle became a necessary accessory in my life.

One day Mum came to give me a hand and we decided to paper a ceiling my first attempt. All went well for the first two strips but the third would not go straight. Matters were made more difficult because we were balanced between a table and a sideboard. The table was a little too low, the sideboard somewhat too high. I suppose we were getting tired. In the middle of our struggles and laughter the door bell rang and, after the fourth ring, I left Mum holding up the paper while I answered the door. It was a man selling apples which we had no money to buy. When I returned Mum was almost wrapped in the paper which was now in several pieces. Time to call a halt and have a nice cup of tea! Several pots of tea later we did finish it and it has always remained one of those funny situations brought out over the years for a laugh.

The folk at my old church in Folkestone rallied to the call and turned out their attics and cupboards to supply all our outstanding needs. I spent my meagre savings on a cooker, washing machine and spin-drier, all second-hand of course. From then on it was really a question of stepping out in faith.

Little by little the house became light and attractive. The babies bedroom was papered with ceiling paper, which someone had given to me. It looked a bit anaemic so, with an odd roll of a pretty flowered paper. I put up a few floral strips. I was delighted with the result. The floors were carpeted with squares from sample books which were kindly donated by a shop in Dover. I spent a long time crawling around the floor, seeking the best effects before sticking them down. The stairs were painted white with a different coloured square on each tread. I thought it looked good because it was original. The squares lasted for the eight years we were there.

The house had the usual sized rooms. It took me some time to get used to the smallness after my previous employment, where the rooms had been so large. I found myself taking work into the garden but, as the atmosphere got lighter and brighter, this feeling of being enclosed gradually left me.

The garden was a joy. Apart from pottering about as a child, I had not had the opportunity to work in a garden before. It was large for a town house but small enough for me to manage. It was a bit neglected but with some hard work and a few packets of seeds, left over from Dad's garden, we turned it into a riot of colour. We grew runner beans and salad crops in the borders to help with the budget. At the bottom of the garden was a large shed that I was allowed to turn into a pram shed.

Slowly the autumn of 1963 turned into the spring of 1964. Six months of hard work creating a really pleasant home out of the bits and pieces that other people did not want. I enjoyed it and look on this period of my life as having been truly worthwhile.

The home was planned to help young unmarried mothers, but financially it could not run on that alone. I found that Nigerian doctors and nurses often needed homes for their children while they completed their training in London. There were many advertisements in newspapers; the weekly rate offered was approximately £4 per child. I answered two adverts, not knowing quite what to expect. Both sets of parents answered and came to visit. I have met some lovely people over the years and many of the parents of Nigerian children visited wearing their national costume. Sometimes they brought a number of friends, often unannounced, but as they always supplied their own food there were no difficulties.

The first two children arrived on 4th May 1964; a boy of two months and a girl of sixteen months. The neighbours were very curious but I heard no complaints, perhaps I was just deaf! I notified my friends at the Putney Mother and Baby Home that we were open and subsequently showed some children's officers and church social workers what we had to offer.

By the end of June we had four little babies, from four to six weeks old when they arrived, plus the original two. I rented a room from my next-door neighbour, had a bell fitted there in case I needed assistance at night, and employed two young ladies to help me. Mum came every week to help, fitting in with our hospital appointments and enabling me to go shopping.

If the unmarried mothers were not working, they were encouraged to come and care for their own babies and to take them out. Their average age was 16 - 17 years. For most of these babies we received twenty-five shillings (£1.25) per week if the mother was working, which was about half their wages. No money was paid if they were out of work.

Some of these babies stayed only a few weeks until their adoption, most remained until their mothers could take them home or made some other arrangements. Some girls did marry their child's father.

We lived very much by faith. The two girls who worked with me had one day off each week, taken together at alternate weekends. Their wages were only £2 per week but there was never enough money to pay them both on Saturday, so the one with the free weekend would be paid and the other waited until parents visited on Sunday. Both girls understood the situation and accepted it, they knew that I would pay them as soon as I could.

The babies were fed on National Dried Milk and orange juice, obtained free from the Children's Welfare Clinic. Going to this clinic was quite a parade, with two or three babies to each pram. This took place every two weeks for weighing, measuring and injections, also to collect enough tins of milk and bottles of orange to last until the next visit.

I remember one dear little soul who hated the clinic; within three minutes he could turn the whole peaceful place into a noisy screaming den. His yells upset every other baby and the nurses as well. It became so embarrassing that I would send him with a helper for a half-hour walk, while we dealt with the rest, only allowing him in for the absolute essentials.

For us a "Full House" was nine. I recall one week when we had eleven, as the children due to go did not and those coming did, but we managed. There was always much coming and going. The law was not so strict in those days.

We paid for what we had or we did not have it: the food for toddlers and staff was often prayed in.

Once, for three days, we lived on mackerel which an Irish neighbour begged us to help her eat. Her husband had been out fishing all night. I am quite sure that today, if I fed children under two on that quantity of mackerel and nothing else, they would become ill but no one suffered any ill effects then.

Another time, when we were wanting, a man from along the road knocked and said that he was clearing his allotment and hoped that we would not be offended by his offer of surplus vegetables. Good thing he did not stay too long or we might have had him in the pot as well!!

The washing machine was a small one with a paddle inside and a hand operated wringer. This poor machine was expected to wash 90 to 100 towelling nappies each day plus the whole weekly washing for thirteen of us. This it did for four years until one day it stopped. When the repair man said it needed a new paddle which would cost £7, I told him I would let him know when I had the money. It was difficult for him to accept that, until then, I would do the washing by hand. Later that night he came back with a new paddle as a gift; he was unable to go to bed with us on his mind.

The old machine did almost another four years before the motor went. This time we washed by hand for a week then, one day, we were called to the front door to take possession of a brand-new machine of the same make and model. I could not believe my eyes as I saw it being wheeled up the front path. We had no advance knowledge of this gift, not only the machine but a whole case of washing powder to go with it. The friend who sent it remained anonymous. We cried tears of thankfulness. It worked as hard as the previous one and lasted ten years.

Chapter 5
Babies and Joanne

During my training at Babies Castle I had learnt about convulsions and epileptic fits, but had never seen any. I had been running the home in Dover for about 18 months when, one evening during bath-time, one of the toddlers began to convulse. Being unprepared I did not immediately recognise it as a fit and thought the child was about to die, especially as the convulsions lessened and the child became floppy and unresponsive. The feeling of total inadequacy that comes over one in situations like this is so engulfing. I could only cry to God for help. By the time the doctor arrived, the child was sleeping peacefully. This was the first of many fits that I have dealt with. Some have really shaken me but I think that this first one was by far the worst, not in its severity but by its sudden onset.

In the first year, two of the babies I looked after were handicapped. The first was supposed to go for adoption and her mother did not wish to see her. Daphne was beautiful with fair curls and lovely blue eyes, a round smiley baby. When she was about six weeks old I took her for a medical for her adoption. The doctor wrote on her form that he thought she was mentally handicapped. I was so angry. I suspected that something was wrong but was not willing to accept such a diagnosis.

I took her to a London hospital where a specialist spent two hours with her. The conclusion was that she had cerebral palsy, would never walk and probably would not talk either. I was shocked and devastated, my beautiful baby was to be just a vegetable not only that but her mother could not or did not want her and neither did the Adoption Agency. Daphne had literally no future. At this point I do not remember ever thinking about long term plans for her.

After a very tiring day I put her to bed, but I did not sleep much that night. I found it difficult to pray, I could only ask, "Why?" By the morning I had decided that doctors were sometimes wrong and that if this child did not make progress, it was not going to be my fault.

We had another baby, Clare, a very normal child, just three weeks younger. I decided that when Clare did something, we had to teach Daphne to do the same. What a struggle! We all worked together and were rewarded over and over again. Daphne became as determined as we were that she would succeed.

When Daphne was about two years old, her mother came to claim her. She was married and her new husband wanted to adopt the little girl. Once, prior to this, some people came to see her with a view to fostering but during their visit she had a fit and they went away. It seemed that God had kept her for her parents. I kept in touch throughout her school days and saw her two or three times. At seven years she was an above average reader and at 11 she went to a grammar school. This was a baby whom I had been advised to put in an institution and forget about!!

The other handicapped baby was just ten days old when she arrived from hospital on Christmas Eve. She had Down's Syndrome, then known as "being a Mongol". I had met another such child of about four years old and had not been at all impressed with her. At that time if anyone had asked me to make my life's work with mentally handicapped children, my answer would definitely have been "NO!". How little we know of God's plans for us.

I agreed to accept this little one only because the mother had no where to take her; without the baby she would be allowed to live at home so this baby, Joanne, joined our family, but only until the mother could make other arrangements for her. I was quite adamant that when two years old she would have to leave.

Joanne weighed 4 lbs 10 ozs, looked quite frail and had a habit of curling backwards with her heels reaching for the back of her head. Her tongue was very large; there did not seem enough room in her mouth for it. Feeding her was a very slow business as she quickly tired and preferred to sleep, sometimes she missed a feed because the one before had taken so long. Her breathing was very shallow and at times I wondered if she was still alive. She never cried during her first month with us.

I discovered that she took more of her feed from a coffee cup and without tiring, so after one month we abandoned the bottle. She made slow progress but like Daphne, she was pushed onward. She eventually walked at two and a half years. Yes, she was and is still with us. I loved her so much that I could not ask her mother to put her in an institution.

In all the years that I have been fostering, there have been a few children with whom I could not cope. One child was a little girl whose mother was a nurse. This child had dreadful bouts of screaming; not temper tantrums and never at night. She had been in hospital for observation and tests but nothing was found. She remained with us for about nine months. As we lived in a terraced house, her screaming caused some problems with the neighbours. I invited the child's mother to take her back to the hospital but she refused. As she visited twice a week and was a nurse, I felt that it was her responsibility.

I had taken her to my doctor and to the children's clinic but, although they examined her every time, they could not suggest anything; she seemed in perfect health. The child was placed in another foster home and I heard, some years later, that she had died of a brain tumour. Could not some of her pain have been alleviated? Did her mother already know? And if so, was it a failing on my part that she could not unburden herself?

One day I remember being out with a large twin pram in which were four babies, two coloured and two white, with a coloured toddler holding onto the side. An elderly lady asked me if they were all mine, to which I replied with a smile, "Yes." She left me shaking her head and muttering, "Oh, you poor soul!"

In the garden we often had up to eight prams holding sleeping babies my neighbours were fascinated by how good the babies were and repeatedly asked why they did not cry. Of course they did from time to time, but the secret was that they were only put in their prams to sleep. After they were fed, they played on the floor or lay in the garden until they showed signs of tiredness, that way they usually slept until the next meal-time.

I found balloons and flowers useful, pinned just out of reach, they would move in the breeze and amuse for a long time. We never left babies to cry as I believe that crying can become a bad habit.

Singing is important in a baby's life. Not the continuous monotony of the radio, records or cassettes, these can be useful in moderation as the child grows, but the voice of the carer singing. Many might say that they cannot sing, but I am sure that the baby will appreciate these sounds of love and, with practice, one can always improve.

On many occasions, when clearing up after a feed, there would be five or six babies lying around the living room. I would say, to no one in particular, "You are a beautiful baby", and all of them would smile or laugh. What a joy they were, if I had enough arms I would have gathered them all up together. They were so individual and each one took my words for themselves alone.

I now see that this is just like my Saviour's love for me. Even in a crowd God knows me as an individual by name, and whatever mess I might make of things, He forgives and continues to love me.

Chapter 6
Cot Death

Before breakfast on the first of April 1966 one of my young helpers came to tell me that one of the babies did not look well. I went at once and found a motionless grey child, still warm. I tried the kiss of life to no avail. The doctor and ambulance men arrived and the child was pronounced dead. It was the mysterious "Cot Death" or Sudden Infant Death Syndrome. I had several rather delicate babies, but this one had been a fit, lively four-month old. It seemed impossible that he had left us so suddenly. The police came and took him away. The next few weeks were a nightmare.

The loss, the self recrimination, going over the day and night before in minute detail, looking for the smallest sign of anything wrong. We had a visit from the Health Visitor the previous afternoon and she had remarked how lovely he looked, he would have won any Baby Show.

The inquest was long, one afternoon each week for a month. It was a very harrowing experience. The Coroner was quite sure that, for a coloured child to die in a foster home, there must have at least been neglect. The case was examined over and over again. Everyone, including the baby's parents, had nothing but praise to offer. The Coroner could not understand what he was hearing.

Throughout the month the weather was as miserable as I was. One of the young ladies working with me was unable to continue, but the other remained faithfully at her work, and my neighbour came in to fill the gap. We had a house full of babies and the work had to continue.

My doctor was very supportive and when I said I would close the home, he persuaded me to wait until after the inquest was over, as he had no doubt as to its conclusion. Mum stayed with me often and all our friends at Church prayed. The only prayer I had was that the Coroner should come and see the home for himself, but this was very unlikely as it was not a thing that was done.

Another problem were the newspapers. Across the front page in large type was "Foster Mother receives £26 per week." This was true and, for an ordinary family, it would be a princely sum. However, the articles did not say that this money paid two wages, three National Insurance Stamps and fed 12. There were no downright lies, but I felt that the insinuations, the misrepresentations and the omissions were very unfair.

On the fourth afternoon of the inquest, when someone else was answering questions, I was sitting there, I suppose in rather a numbed state almost beyond listening, and became aware of a lovely warm feeling. I realized that I was sitting in a ray of sunlight coming from a small window high in the roof. At that moment I was absolutely certain that all would be well.

Presently the Coroner turned to me and said, "Now we will visit your establishment, and next week we will meet here at the same time." I was so pleased that the Lord had answered my prayer; the home would speak for itself.

In no way was the house prepared for the Coroner's visit as we did not know he was coming. I was pleased to show him around. When we arrived there were two babies crying, I explained that because I was not there the feeds were late. He said that it was so clean and bright and the children looked well and happy.

The following week the inquest was closed with a verdict of accidental death. In his summing-up the Coroner said that he was very impressed and that he did not know how we had managed to do so much with our £26 per week. This did not receive headline news, but I was so thankful that it was finished.

It took some time for things to return to normal, people were embarrassed when they met me and did not want to talk. For a long time I was nervous about the health of the babies and would wander about at night, looking at them and listening to their breathing. Slowly my self-assurance returned. Daily I was lifted up in prayer by so many friends, my strength came from the Lord. Alone I would not have had the confidence to continue. Babies need constant attention and, in spite of all, the work went on. My life was there with those little ones.

Chapter 7
Disabilities and Help

There were still many mothers who wanted to keep their babies but had no immediate way to solve their problems of home and finance. The work continued in Dover for another four years after our tragedy. During those years in Dover, fifty-one children came through our front door. Some stayed just a week, others for several years and some a lifetime.

We had a very big two year old, Simon, with a hare lip even so he was a beautiful child with very blond hair, large blue eyes and a happy nature. The lip was repaired, so successfully that it hardly showed. Simon was a good companion for Joanne and spent time jumping her up and down in her baby-bouncer, which was hooked onto a door frame or onto a large tripod that Mr Baker had made for her in the garden. Simon's mother married and, after little more than a year with us, he was able to go home.

Two little Indian girls were brought by their father, to stay while their mother was in hospital. The older child, of three and a half years, spoke a few words of English and would try to translate for her two year old sister. On the day they arrived we were having a party to celebrate Joanne's second birthday and of course jelly was on the menu. These two little Indians were horrified because it wobbled nothing could persuade them to try it.

Every morning when I called them, the older one would tell the little one to get up. On the fourth morning I thought that I would be clever and say what I thought the older child had said. I was not prepared for what happened next. They both fell out of bed and rolled on the floor laughing, they giggled and giggled all the while they were dressing. Was it what I had said or was it my accent? Perhaps both! When the mother was better, the parents came to fetch their children. They were very pleased with the amount of English their children had learned in just one month. It seems so easy for small children to learn another language, and they are not at all shy about it.

One little fellow, Barry, was born prematurely. His mother had to leave him in hospital and, for several reasons, did not visit him as often as she should have done. Consequently, when she came to take Barry home, they were strangers. He cried in his unfamiliar surroundings and his mother was nervous. He was difficult to feed, so did not get enough and screamed loud and long. The neighbours complained about the screaming and the baby was taken back to the hospital. Throughout the next six months Barry went home three times; finally he screamed every time his mother approached him. She was discouraged and depressed, unable to cope with him and her unhelpful neighbours. She loved him but said he would have to go into care as he could not stay in hospital any longer.

Barry was eleven months old when he came to us. A transparent white colour, with no muscular tone at all, and no interest in anything. He hung in the baby-bouncer like a rag doll. I suspended it in the doorway that I used the most, so as to have every possible contact with him. Joanne could not understand why Barry did not move, and took it upon herself to jump him up and down just as Simon had played with her two years before.

A month later his mother came to visit and found him so changed. We worked out a plan for visiting so that she could really get to know him and care for him. After three months he was getting around the floor on all fours, could pull himself up by a chair, was learning to feed himself and had become a friendly little boy I invited his mother for a long week-end so that she could take over his care for four days. As we sat chatting on the Sunday evening, she said that she felt confident enough to take Barry home. I was so pleased because, as she was expecting again, I felt that this boy might not have a place if he did not get home before the new baby arrived Barry had stayed with us for just four months. I heard later that the new baby had arrived and all was well.

We were still receiving a few babies destined for adoption. One little girl was Anglo-french. She came at six weeks old whilst her adoption formalities were finalised. All the clothes in her suitcase had been handmade, about seven sets of everything, beautifully knitted with nighties and dresses all hand embroidered It was all so lovely that we repacked it and passed it on to the adopters as it was. I had the privilege of taking her to London. I was not allowed to meet the adoptive family, but I could hear them. There were three little boys all suitably impressed with her; it was love at first sight. Their father was still trying to park the car but they had what they came for and were eager to go.

Another little boy whom we took for a month was the youngest of seven. His mother needed an operation and Dad did not feel he could manage the baby, the only one not at school. The family lived in two rooms and the water was four floors below. The child was spotlessly clean, and not just cleaned up to come. How did that mother manage so well? I had the pleasure to meet some of this family when it was time for the little one to leave. They were so happy to be reunited.

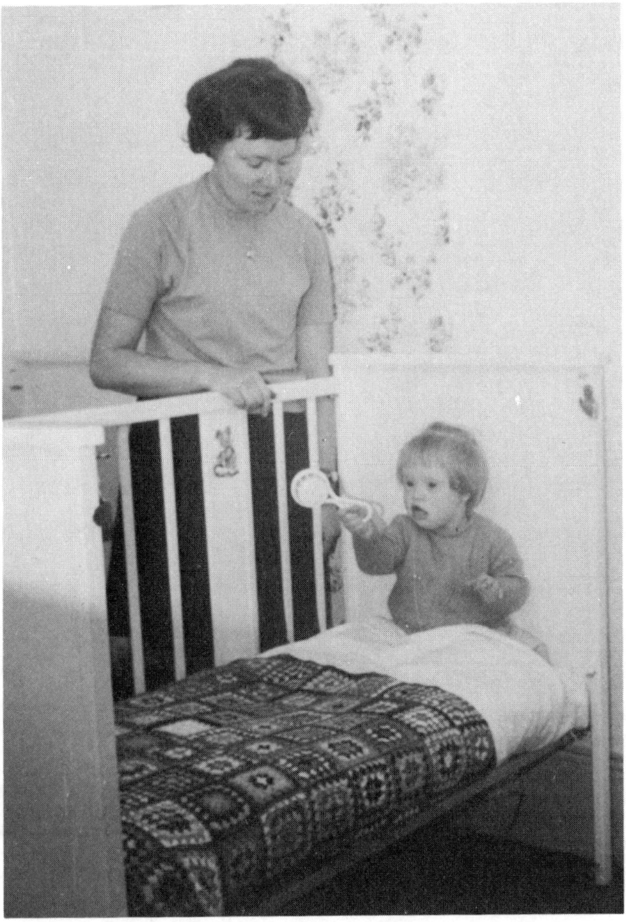

One of the bedrooms, Dover

CHAPTER 8
CHRISTOPHER

During my last two years at Dover, things changed dramatically. The Abortion Law was passed and the allowances for unmarried mothers improved. The mothers had less need to work and more kept their babies. Our numbers dwindled, at one point to only Joanne.

Around that time the newspapers were reporting several cases of gross overcrowding and neglect in some foster homes, and a move was made to limit the numbers. Our registration number was set at four with an overlap to five.

I had one young lady in her teens working for me then, but with only Joanne I could not afford to pay her. She insisted on staying, she said that as long as our National Insurance Cards were stamped she would be happy to stay and would do a correspondence course to fill in the time. I was pleased to have her company and did some renovating during the lull.

This situation did not last very long. I received a call from a Children's Department in London requesting a place for a severely handicapped Down's boy. He was five weeks old, had a congenital heart condition and was blind. I could not say "No", I had three empty beds. A week later we were introduced to Christopher. First impressions were of a cuddly bundle, with fair hair standing straight up from his head for about three inches. Joanne promptly claimed him as her own, she fetched and carried and was always attentive to his needs.

I wrote to the RNIB to gain as much information as I could about the care of a blind baby. They sent me a lovely letter and some useful pamphlets, but they thought that, with all the problems involved, I should not have high hopes. The doctor said that Christopher would not live the year out and not to love him too much or I would be hurt. In spite of many set backs he did survive that first year and is still with us.

Christopher really enjoyed music and at nine months could already tap to rhythm. He could not sit up, he did not have the balance for that until he was two years old. Soon after his first birthday Christopher had tonsillitis and had an epileptic fit which lasted on and off for about an hour. He was taken into hospital and put on phenobarbitone and other drugs with which he was treated until he was eleven years old. This I think really held up his speech, he only managed some indistinct words which few people could understand.

By two and a half years he could play several little tunes on the piano and was beginning to shuffle about on his bottom. I was always patching trousers. From there he learnt to roll over and laboriously haul himself along with his arms, lying flat on his front. This method of travel lasted for about two years. He was always dirty and, because of his drugs, he dribbled profusely. I thought he was never going to progress. But eventually his legs grew stronger and he went about on hands and knees for another two years; a little less dirty. He was admitted to hospital at least three times each winter with chest infections, often not expected to survive. The years passed and he grew, very slowly, but the infections left him weak, and his progress was extremely slow.

Just after Christopher came, Mark arrived. He was of Jamaican origin and also registered blind, with some spasticity down his left side. As Mark grew we had to come to terms with his strange vision, caused by Optic Atrophy. He could pick up a Smartie but would crash into a door or wall. He gave himself some very bad bruises. He had repeated ear infections. These would come on very suddenly and he spent many miserable nights in pain. His sight was so poor, Mark would quickly lose us in an open space. He could move at great speed and was extremely active. When he thought that he was lost, he would howl as loudly as possible until we fetched him, then in two or three minutes he would be gone again. For a time we stopped going to the park and the beach; it was just too exhausting running after him. We had always enjoyed our days out and felt deprived. Going to the park or beach cost us nothing but the effort to get there. I had to solve Mark's problem for all our sakes. I tried attaching him to a long length of clothes-line tied to the pram and taught him to find his way back along the rope. He was fascinated by this and very proud when he succeeded, so much happier than when he ran free and was content with it for a long time. While attached to his rope, I taught him to come to my voice. By the end of the summer he had gained confidence in his new found abilities and no longer needed his rope.

Mark's brother, Andrew, had been in care all his life. He had many homes during his short four years and was showing signs of becoming very disturbed. When the Child Care Officer asked me to take him, I was happy to do so. He settled down and fitted into the family well. As he was six months older than Joanne, she benefited from his company. One evening, just after he had started school, he awoke crying. I went to see what was wrong and found him standing up on his top bunk, insisting that a chicken had flown down the back of his bed. We had to pull the bed out and look under the mattress before he was satisfied that it was no longer there. His teacher had been reading the story of "Chick-a-licken"!

One day, when Andrew was at school, I decided to treat myself to a trip around the supermarket, small of course by today's standards. I usually had too many children to embark on such a venture. I sat Christopher and Mark in the trolley and Joanne trotted alongside. I was suitably impressed by the choice and layout; my shopping was done in the corner shop where the goods were limited to those things that most people needed. There were great stacks of tins towering up from the floor. Joanne had been brought up to be tidy and she picked up a tin to give to me. I was just in time to snatch her away as an avalanche descended, making the most dreadful noise. This was followed by a silence as everyone turned towards us. Very red in the face, I apologised to no-one in particular, looked at the heap of tins, decided there was nothing I could do about it and hurried away. We spent a little more time and selected a few items before checking out. While I was paying, Joanne managed to upset another stack. I could not get away quickly enough; it was several years before I set foot in one of those stores again. By that time the stacks of tins had disappeared, too dangerous I should think.

A treat for us was to take a packed lunch to Kersney Abbey Gardens. We walked past the Paper Mill, the Old Mill and on through the village. This took us along the river and into the back entrance of the gardens. Here we often saw dragon-flies and sometimes small furry creatures creeping about. There was space to run and play ball; a children's playground; ducks on the lake and in summer - ice creams! My favourite times were on the warm days in winter. Then we would take hot soup and sit just long enough to eat it. Christopher's best part of the outing was going under the railway arch. He discovered the echo when he was quite young and, in spite of his lack of sight, knew just when to make a noise.

Christopher and Mark were both frightened of animals. I thought that perhaps we should have a dog and talked to our doctor about it. He suggested a Dachshund, as, of the small dogs, they were probably the best with children.

The first dog we had was very good. She just moved away when she had enough attention. She liked our outings and, on the all day ones, would end up in the pram with the boys. They never made a fuss of her, but tolerated her well.

Chapter 9
Joanne at School

Through the Health Visitor we were referred to Dr Ludlow's Playgroup at River. The transport was provided. The group was run by a band of volunteers. It was as much help to the mothers as to the children. At that time the attitude towards handicapped children was that they should be put away. Handicapped adults and children were not seen as individuals, but lumped together as a whole group for whom little or nothing could be done.

This was the first constructive help I received for my little family and I found it very encouraging. Here was a group of people who not only agreed that a lot could be done, but were willing to help me do it. Until then I had only my common sense and intuition to guide me. What a lot of trial and error! Now I could discuss and plan ahead.

At the age of four and a half, Joanne was at a Nursery School for two mornings each week. People were inclined to leave her to do what she wanted, not expecting her to join in with the group. They did not credit her with any understanding and she was clever enough to play on that. Two afternoons each week I ran a play-group at home for the under-fives in our street. It was quite successful. The children did the usual pre-school things and it gave me a point of contact with my neighbours. This went on until Joanne started school and I had no more time.

Education for Mentally Handicapped children was non-existent but there were day care centres that children like Joanne could attend. Our nearest one was in Folkestone. The special bus for it would pass on the main road, about 20 minutes walk away, at approximately 8.00 am and return about 4.00 pm. At this time I was working alone with the four children, the two blind ones not walking or feeding themselves. Joanne and Christopher were still very delicate and we would have had to have been on-route by 7.30 am in all weathers. The special bus visited all the villages along the Alkam Valley and was not guaranteed to arrive at school before 9.30 am. Joanne had mastered the art of being clean and dry, but I did not think that she could hold out for more than two hours. From what I heard, the timing of the bus was erratic. All things considered, the day centre did not seem to be what we required so I declined the place offered.

As Andrew was attending the local Infants School at the end of our road, I applied for a place for Joanne. My application was turned down because Joanne "would not learn to read"; so I set about teaching her. If that was how she would get into school, we would do our best to oblige!

During the previous six years in Dover, I had a number of young girls and a few volunteers working for me. Some ladies from the Methodist Church came to baby-sit every other Sunday evening. Jean, the daughter of one of these ladies, became a great friend. When she was not doing her homework, she was often in our house feeding and bathing the babies. By the time Joanne was five years old, Jean was a qualified teacher in the school at the end of the road. When Jean heard about Joanne learning to read, she was very enthusiastic and encouraging. She borrowed books from school and I began, using the "Look and See" method. Joanne was very keen and progressed well. I used home-made word-cards to be sure that she had learnt the words correctly.

The following year I applied again for a place in the school, stating that Joanne could now read four books of the reading scheme being used and as she could dress herself completely, she would not take up the teachers time. She was given a small test and got her place. It still seems hard to me that to get a place in school, Joanne had to learn to read first.

Joanne suffered a lot in the playground. When I discovered that she was being dragged around by her ponytail, I cut her hair short at once. As I could not teach her to be aggressive, she was not good at defending herself.

In the beginners class she started with the advantage of reading and self-help. She had the benefit of nursery school, which was not so common in those days, and had worked with many educational toys. She could count and knew her colours, but she could not learn at the same speed as her classmates. With the help of my friend Jean, I did what I could at home, but, over the next eighteen months, Joanne gradually slipped from being ahead to being behind in her class. She was perfectly happy and loved school. I knew that if she was to learn she would need special teaching in a much smaller class. But where?

Joanne benefited greatly from those eighteen months and made many friends. Like all parents, I had tried to teach her not to talk to or go with strangers, but did not know how much she was able to understand. By nature Down's Syndrome children are very friendly and this renders them vulnerable. As time progressed I stopped meeting Joanne at the school gate and would wait by the first crossing, giving her a little independence. One day my mother went to meet her and Joanne was very late in coming. A friend's father saw Joanne struggling because the elastic in her tights had broken. He suggested that he should bring her in his car but she answered very firmly, "Auntie Jeanne said NO". Kindly he did not insist but came to tell me. By this time she had met my mother. Joanne had certainly understood my warning and had enough strength of character to act on it.

Joanne in the garden at Dover

Chapter 10
Holidays in Broadstairs

When Joanne was about four years old, I discovered that children in care could have a holiday allowance. What joy, we could go away. It would be quite an undertaking with two children aged four years and two blind boys of just two years, also we had no transport. My childhood memories of holidays in Broadstairs came flooding back. I wrote for a Holiday Guide, decided June would be a good month before it became too busy, and booked a Guest House not far from the sea and a chalet on the beach at Viking Bay and contacted St Mary's Children's Home to ask for the loan of a large pram, so that Christopher could sleep on the beach. Although he was two years old, he could not sit up for long and tired very quickly.

Now how could we get there? My friend Joan had a small car but we were five, and, besides the luggage containing terry nappies for two, we had to have the twin pushchair - no buggies in those days! I was reluctant to ask her. Mr Baker offered his services and I decided that, if he took the pushchair to the station, I could take the rest by taxi. Mr Baker accompanied us on the train journey and to the guest house, it worked but was exhausting. We said good-bye to Mr Baker who promised to come back for us in two weeks and to visit us the following week-end.

The guest house was large, drab and empty, but we would not be in very much and if the children did make a mess, there was little to spoil. The chalet on the sands was very good, with water and a gas ring. We installed ourselves and fetched the pram.

I was able to heat soup and Christopher's dinners, also do the washing and drying down there. Mark often managed to get into the sea with all his clothes on, once including his anorak, so I was more than pleased to have somewhere to hang things.

It was June and, although the weather was not very reliable, on the fine days the beach became really crowded. I pinned the chalet number onto the backs of the children's costumes in case they should stray; with so many people it was hard to keep track of the children? One day I lost Joanne; in about twenty minutes most of the people on the beach were looking for her. Eventually I found her sitting on the pot in the chalet singing quietly to herself. Andrew and Joanne made friends with two little girls on the beach and most days they came to visit us and play.

The food at the Guest House was not good; mostly out of tins and, when served, dried round the edges. No one else but us was there. It was not satisfactory, but, I now knew that I could take my four children on holiday because they were socially acceptable and would not spoil anyone else's vacation. I had been able to cope with the washing, the midday meal, and manage the wet days.

Our first holiday came to an end and we were pleased to go home when Mr Baker came to fetch us. But I was already looking forward to next year. The journey home must have been uneventful because I do not remember it.

The following year I found a guest house run by a lovely Christian lady. Not only did she take children, she would welcome mine. Arthur, another friend we had made during the year through selling cards from Mencap, offered to transport us in the Deal Ambulance for Mentally Handicapped People. This was just what we needed as it allowed us to take all the extra bits and pieces to make life easier. Christopher still needed to sleep during the day and to have his cot at night.

Arthur helped us down to the beach. I left him with the children and went to fetch the chalet key as it needed my signature. During that first night Joanne was very sick, it was bubbly and smelt of soap. I was puzzled but by the morning she was better and ate breakfast as usual. Later that morning Andrew found an empty bubble pot on the beach and lamented loudly that Joanne had drunk it all yesterday,

Once we went into a chemist in Charlotte Street, and Andrew insisted in a loud voice that, "It smells like lions in here!" So embarrassing!

The landlady was smashing; she did so many things to make our stay happy and made life easier for me. She allowed the two little ones to eat their evening meal in pyjamas and served our meal before the other guests arrived. The little ones were very tired, having been on the beach all day, and needed their beds. She would bring us a packed lunch during the morning and have a coffee with me, I really appreciated that. At the end of our stay she invited us to return the following year and we accepted.

The two little girls whom the children had made friends with the year before were also on holiday and, with the very good weather, a lovely time was had by all.

Chapter 11
Moving to Broadstairs

We were fast outgrowing our flat in Dover. Now that I had two children at school full time, I felt I could do more. There was a great need for homes for handicapped children. This was evident by the number of phone calls I was receiving each week, from all over the country, asking for places.

Although Joanne was in a normal Infants school, I knew that she would never be able to cope in a Junior school. Also there was the education of Mark, now aged four years, and Christopher, aged three and a half, to be considered. This was not pressing but months turned into years and Dover had no facilities. We would have to move but, with £30 in the bank, the prospect seemed somewhat remote. I prayed incessantly about the situation and wrote many letters to various organisations. Help was not forth coming as it was the year of the elderly, and all funds were already earmarked for their various projects.

By now my landlord, Mr Baker, had become a family friend. He offered to sell the house we were in and to lend me the money to buy a larger property. He would move with us into a flat and, for the next five years until he retired, would work in the house for his weekly expenditure, his mid-day meal, laundry and cleaning. We went to a solicitor to have the agreement drawn up correctly. This was a good experience for me as it was the first time that I needed to do anything legally. Mr Baker and I did it together. I was able to ask questions and learned much subsequently I have had no problems with other transactions.

Now where to start looking? Eastbourne and Thanet had the type of schools that we might need. My first choice was Broadstairs; not only was I attracted by the town, but it was within easy reach by train.

The house that we required would need living accommodation for myself and up to eight children; a flat for Mr Baker and a flat for my parents. My mother had arthritis and, although she was still quite active, she would eventually need care. My sister had been living in my parents house but would not be joining us as she felt that she would like more freedom. We viewed several properties; two had structural faults; some were too small; the ones that were large enough were too expensive.

One house in particular kept being offered to us. I did not want to look at it as the sale price was £11,000 and we had only £8,000. Eventually Mr Baker went to see it and came back with a glowing report. I resisted for two more weeks but no other houses were offered to us. I could not see the point of going to view this house when there was no way in which we could buy it. After much discussion my parents and I made the trip to Broadstairs. The house was ideal, just what we needed and I had a vision of how it could be when we lived there. On arriving home I was able to take pencil and paper and draw how it could be split up to accommodate us all.

Of course I prayed for this dream, but with no real faith of being able to raise that sort of money; anyway it was more money than I could visualize - an enormous sum. After two days the estate agent rang to ask what I thought. I said it was just what I wanted but the price was way beyond my means. When I told him that the most I could raise was £8,500 and that was really scraping the barrel, there was a silence. Then he said, "Offer it anyway." I did and the next day the offer was accepted. The Lord showed once again His wonderful way. There we were busily praying for the money, but that was not God's method.

During our last six months in Dover I had been so sure we were destined to move, that I accepted almost any item offered to me. The furniture in my four small rooms would not go far in a larger house. As we had so little money, we economized by doing our own packing. We tied the boxes securely and colour coded them for each floor. This proved to be very useful both for the removal men and for ourselves afterwards. One room on each floor was designated for boxes which had been briefly marked with their contents

Moving Day, 4th July 1970, dawned bright and sunny, promising to be hot. The removal van arrived at 7.00 am. Mr Baker left soon afterwards on his moped, to arrive before the vendors left and to collect the keys. The removal van was not large enough and a second one had to be fetched. Apart from that all went smoothly. A friend had given me a fruit cake and with slices of it plus cups of tea, the men were sustained throughout the day.

The vans left before lunchtime. Andrew and Joanne were at school. As this was a busy day for me, it seemed the best solution. I swept up and had a picnic lunch with the two little boys before taking them to the hospital for Christopher's last appointment with the paediatrician. My friend Jean collected the children from school and had tea with us, after which we piled into another friend's car for the journey to Broadstairs. I thought that most of the things had gone in the vans but I kept finding items. Once again the twin push-chair took up most of the boot, but with some rearranging we all got in, including the dog!

I locked the door on the life I had known for eight very mixed years; there had been trauma and grief but, taken as a whole, they were eight most enjoyable years which I am so pleased I had. I had arrived with many things that people had so willingly given me, but without any money, I was leaving in much the same way, but now we were five.

The evening was very hot and the children were tired. It was a most uncomfortable journey. My thoughts raced during those inactive moments. I had been happy in Dover, why had I wanted to change all that? What would happen if I could not pay back the money that I owed? Would I make friends? What was Mr Baker doing? and so on . . .

When we arrived at about 6.30 pm the first van was still being unloaded. There had been road works on the Toll Bridge at Sandwich and the road had been closed for several hours. The men were most helpful and put up the children's beds in one room so that I could tuck them in. Even in their strange surroundings, they were soon asleep. The removal was certainly not over-charged even for those days. I paid only £26 for five men and two vans for the whole day, and not a cross word!

July 4th had been so hot, but on July 5th it was cold and raining. Perhaps we were cold because of the large, strange surroundings. Here we were in our new home, Lynton House.

Mr Baker and I had a good look around, everywhere was so dirty. After my four small rooms it was difficult to know where to begin. In every room, including the bathroom, there were gas taps on the floors and walls. None of the windows would open as the joints had been painted over. Mr Baker's first task was to wire the gas taps to pieces of wood, so that little fingers would not be able to play with them. Next he eased open the windows to air the rooms, more than necessary in some of them! The dog behaved very strangely in the hall. When I investigated, I found an electric socket with no cover on it. As the two boys were still at the crawling stage, they could easily have had a nasty shock. My first job had to be in the kitchen as there were maggots crawling in the cupboards.

We thought we had a hot water system but it did not work and a plumber pronounced it beyond repair. It was not until four months later, in October, that a new hot water system and central heating were installed. In the scullery was a large stone sink which sufficed for bathing the children. The rest of us had to make do with a wash-down in a baby bath. We did not know anyone so we had to manage.

After paying the removal men, I had £1.50 to feed five of us, and provide Mr Baker's mid-day meal, for a whole month. My little supply of stores soon began to dwindle. I asked around and found a small grocer in St Peter's where I could have a monthly account, with delivery included. This was how I had managed at Dover; it suited me well as I was paid every four weeks. If the shopkeeper had known of my financial state, he may not have been inclined to serve me. However, he was well rewarded as over the next four years our family grew and we became good customers.

The kitchen was built onto the side of the house. The previous owners had left the gas cooker. As there was no electricity, apart from the light, it was a real blessing to have that cooker. But oh the disasters! Not being used to gas, I was so pleased to hand the cooking over to Mum when she arrived at the end of the month. The nearest electric plug was in the hall and the fridge had to be plugged in there. The larder was beyond the scullery.

Those first days were really exhausting, by nine o'clock we were all asleep in bed. After cleaning the few rooms needed for our use, I set about preparing my parent's rooms. When they arrived we had some more furniture, their house having been larger than their new flat.

As it was nearing the end of term, I left schooling until the new school year. The two six year old's were most helpful during those early days; fetching and carrying, and unpacking boxes. Joanne went exploring and locked herself in one of the attic rooms. I had thoughts of calling the Fire Brigade. It was a long time before we could get her to understand that she should push the key under the door so that we could unlock it from the outside. We then removed all keys from the doors.

Curtains were the biggest problem as the windows here were so much larger, and there were so many of them. In most rooms the curtains could only be hung across the lower part of the windows. It did not look very good but we could not afford any new ones.

The garden was a wilderness and had a large lawn which could have been a tennis court. We all helped to cut it using an old push and pull lawn mower. As we had to be self-sufficient, we needed a larger vegetable plot. Mr Baker would water six square feet of grass evening and morning and I dug it up later in the day.

This was very hard work and it took a long time to remove almost half the lawn.

A lady from the local Methodist Church visited us, she lived nearby. As we had attended the Methodist Church in Dover, it seemed right for us to join the one here in York Street. Joanne and Andrew were soon members of the Sunday School.

CHAPTER 12
LYNTON HOUSE

About the same time as my parent's arrival, I accepted a brother and sister, Carl and Greta, from the local children's department.

The little girl was five years old and very talkative. We heard a lot about her past although I doubt if it was all as she told us. She said her mother did not make toast as I did. I thought that perhaps her mother had an electric toaster but no, "She only made it by scraping off the black"!! There were many meals that these two did not like, or maybe had never had. Most times, when I said that I had made something especially good for them, they would try a little and after a few weeks were eating everything. Greta was very domesticated, she often helped and worked very well. Mum and I imagined her in later years, surrounded by children, leaning on the garden gate talking. These children came to us because their family became homeless, they were able to rejoin their parents a year later when the family was given a council house.

With Thanks

Playing games, Lynton House

With Thanks

Mum and Dad

My parents had brought extra beds but when my niece and nephew came to stay, the camp beds came in to use as well. It was a fairly warm summer and one blanket each had to suffice, doubled in half if it was cold. We managed with sheets by folding those for the smaller children to make top and bottom from one, and washing them only on the days when we knew they would dry. We still had no hot water but the washing machine was the open top type and did the job well.

At the beginning of August we were eight children and four adults. As Mum had taken over in the kitchen, I was able to concentrate on the summer holidays. The promenade at Stone Bay was under construction but, apart from heaps of sand, nothing much was happening at our end. We spent most days on the beach, the piles of sand adding to the fun. We ate every possible meal outdoors, working on the principle that the less we were in, the less work we would need to do.

We seemed to be the only ones using the beach, all that fresh air and sunshine was free. The children were full of life, a beautiful, healthy colour and tired out at the end of each day. They wore only pants. We did not have any bathing costumes apart from the one my niece brought with her and she "lived" in that. Wearing no clothes cut down on the washing and ironing and that was fine by me. We still did not know anyone and only had a few visitors that first year.

At the end of August we said good-bye to my niece and nephew who were returning to my sister in Maidstone to start school again. Joanne was given a place at Stone Bay School, which was for children with severe learning difficulties. By now a move was being made towards providing education for these children, but it was to be a number of years before their right to education was recognised, and enough teachers were trained to do the work.

We were asked to take a little Down's Syndrome girl of five months, she had lived in a Nursery before coming to us. This made four children under school age. Andrew and Greta would both need a normal Infant's School. There were two from which I could choose; both had a good reputation, both were a long way from us. I chose the one which had no main roads to cross, thinking that, in time, the children could come part of the way home alone. My bicycle was dusted off and came into its own again, it cut down the time if I could ride one way. Dad liked a walk and would often take them in the mornings. Mr Baker was happy to collect Joanne in the afternoons. Mum looked after the little ones and we established a routine.

Joanne soon learnt to go and come home alone as her school was in our road and on the same side. After a while we left the other two at the end of the footpath, to go in with the other children. One Monday morning Andrew put his dinner money under a bush along the footpath. He told his teacher but it could not be found. When I asked him about it, he said that he wanted to see if it would grow and was going to get it on his way home!

By now the evenings were beginning to draw in. We had a few portable heaters but, in those large rooms, they did not do much. We doubled the blankets and used our dressing gowns; even some of the curtains that had been too small became bed covers. There was no money to buy anything as every available penny was put towards the central heating, due to be installed in October. Even so I had to borrow more money from Mr Baker as the heating and hot water were really essential now. You can imagine the bliss of that first hot bath in a lovely warm bathroom after so long!

We prayed about the bedding and waited, not in vain. One of Mum's artist friends in Folkestone rang to say that her elderly mother had died and, in the loft, she had found her mother's trousseau. Would we like it and could she bring it that same day? She knew no one else to ask. What I expected and what arrived just had to be seen. There was nothing missing and for the most part it was new, even pillows. We are still using some of the towels today. No half measures, our prayers had been answered in full.

I continued to dig up part of the lawn for vegetables and the rest of the garden became less like a wilderness. At the bottom of the garden we found a beautiful pond, all overgrown. This presented a new problem and we were obliged to put a fence around the remaining lawn, to prevent swimming expeditions! The ground floor was very dark with the trees all overgrown a bit like Sleeping Beauty's castle. It made such a difference once they were cut back.

During the first year at Lynton House, a large store in Cliftonville closed down and I was able to buy curtain material at 50p per yard; for some of the rooms we needed fifteen yards. The patterns were not those I would have picked, but at that price I could not be too choosey. Mum's treadle machine flew into action and at last we had neat looking windows.

Mum and I worked together for that first year. Dad did the garden and Mr Baker put back all those things that "came off in our hands", and made numerous articles that made our lives easier. Amongst other things, he showed me how to burn off the thick layers of paint without catching the house alight. I had already done a great deal of painting and papering in the previous house so, once the paint was off and the hours of sandpapering done, the rest was easy.

In 1972 we had the fire precaution work done on the first floor and took the opportunity to make some of the rooms smaller, and acquired a linen room. With seven children, four adults plus my niece and nephew every holiday, that was a real blessing. It gave Mum somewhere to sew without having to keep clearing away, and me somewhere to do the ironing.

One year later we engaged our first member of staff. Now Mum was able to take up her oil painting again, although we were still grateful to have her help at bedtimes. This member of staff, Helen, was a severe diabetic. I knew nothing about this condition but was to learn a great deal over the next few years. Helen had many disappointments in her short working life. As soon as she had a reaction, due to lack of sugar, her employers and work mates took fright and she lost one job after another, until her self-image was so low that she was treated for depression. I also was frightened when I found her unconscious, but her work was good and I felt that such a strong, healthy young woman should not live the life of an invalid. She seemed to have bad patches when things kept going wrong and it would be difficult to stabilize her, but once stabilised she could have a good spell of up to two years. Close working relationships have to be worked at like all relationships, and we had our ups and downs. There were some very good times during the 12 years that Helen stayed with our family.

By now Mum and Dad were installed in their flat on the ground floor. I tried to obtain a grant for a bathroom for them but this was refused because the bathroom would be across the hall from their flat. It seemed a flimsy argument but, eventually, we were able to install one ourselves.

A sudden downpour or rain would produce a drama as we had several places which flooded. The drive sloped towards the house and, as there was only a very shallow step, the front hall was often covered with water. I bailed up the water outside the front door using a sand bucket and carried it through the house to the back. After months of bailing, sometimes at night, I had made quite a hole in a corner. A slate became visible and when I pulled it up, there was a perfectly good drain. How or why it had been covered I did not know, but I was so pleased to have found it. Two other places leaked but were not repaired for some time and, as they were in the roof, this proved rather costly.

During the first few months after our arrival in Broadstairs, Christopher caught measles. What with his rash and heart condition he was almost a purple colour. We had signed on with an elderly doctor who had a small practice. Christopher had some bad experiences during his early years and was very nervous of strangers, and the medical profession in general. This doctor visited us twice a day for a few days and took the time to talk and play with Christopher. From then onwards, Christopher slowly became less afraid but it was many years before he was really confident. This helpful attitude was continued by our second family doctor who was always pleased to see Christopher and showed great patience and kindness, not only with Christopher but with all my family.

When we first visited the dentist it was just to say, "Hello." Having taught Christopher to open his mouth "ever so wide", he would do so, right by the front door. We progressed from there, through the waiting room, to the surgery; there Christopher stood with his back to the surgery door. At no time did the dentist hurry him. What patience! It was many years before Christopher agreed to sit in the dentist's chair or to tolerate any instruments in his mouth. Finally, at the age of twenty years, he went confidently with the dentist, sat in the chair, and had his teeth cleaned. So any parents having problems, do not lose heart, it can get better!

Mark and Christopher were now five years old. Mark was able to start at Stone Bay School, with Joanne, but for Christopher it was more difficult. He was not walking and was very small for his age - wearing size two shoes and age two trousers at six years old. It was not unusual for him to wet ten to twelve pairs of trousers in a day. It was impossible to train him using pinned nappies, there were no disposable ones then, so I made him terry pants which now can be easily purchased. Eventually Christopher started school, at six and a half, at a special unit in the grounds of Lanthorne Hospital, Broadstairs. Some of the children were day pupils and were taken there by taxi, the others lived in the hospital. Christopher found it hard to leave the familiar surroundings of home but, with a lot of help from his teachers, he gradually settled down. One day an old style London taxi went to the school to collect him. He took fright and arrived home in a state of total exhaustion, soaking wet with perspiration.

Chapter 13
The Farm

In 1973 I heard of a farm with five huts in an orchard where we could take the children for a holiday. I booked one for a week, not wanting to commit myself too much. The hut consisted of a large bedroom with sleeping space for five, and a living room with a cooker, a sink with cold water, and sleeping places for two. A bucket toilet was round the back.

It was decided that Mum and Dad would stay at home and enjoy the quiet; my niece and nephew would bring their tent and we would take two cots. As it would be difficult for two of us to cope with nine children in a strange place, I rang the labour exchange to see if they had someone to help us. They had, and, within a few hours a very ample young woman came to see me. Time was short, about two days before we were due to leave for the farm, so, without too many questions, I engaged her.

On arriving at the farm we found there was one bed short but as one of them was a large double bed, we turned it sideways against the wall and slept three of the smaller children across its length. They all had sleeping bags and looked like three little bugs; we used this method for an extra place on several other holidays.

Our extra helper was a heavy smoker. I refused to have smoking inside the hut as there was a great deal of wood about and several of the children suffered from severe bronchitis. Work was not really in her line but she was another pair of eyes and, as she propped up the wall outside puffing on her cigarette, she would tell us if someone was missing or in trouble. Every now and again I managed to jolt her into action, but mostly only at meal times. However the weather was splendid and the week passed quickly. We had surmounted all the difficulties - borrowing a mini-bus and driver, dispatching my permanent helper with the four most able-bodied children on the train. (Hooray for British Rail! We could buy one adult ticket and the four children could travel for 50p or was it £1? I cannot remember but it certainly helped the budget.)

Everyone enjoyed the farm, they were all healthy and brown. All the effort that was put into arriving and leaving made a week too short. Now we knew that we could cope, we would come for two weeks next year.

The farm was what older readers will know as a small holding. A flock of sheep, three goats with their kids, geese with goslings, two or three horses, chickens, cats and dogs. Alongside was a market garden with green-houses and fruit trees.

We have returned to the farm every year since. For several years, in the beginning, we picked raspberries for an hour or so and in return had enough for our dinner. We could buy many of our vegetables from the farm, the rest of our supplies we bought at the village shop. On some holidays we were as many as nineteen, using two huts. One year we took four cots, three push-chairs - one a twin chair - and 250 disposable nappies, which were all cut by hand from rolls before we left and disposed of on a bonfire every day. On late holidays we picked blackberries and made jam. Our cooking was done on two gas rings using bottled gas.

Once, in the days before we had our own transport, a very kind lady, who worked in the Christian Book Depot in Kennington, showed an interest in the family and hired a minibus, with a driver, for the day and took us to a forest. The children had never been to a forest and, at first, were nervous of the trees but soon gained confidence and we had a most enjoyable day.

The orchard was used by sheep which, with our non-walkers, could have presented a problem, but the lady who owned the farm was very understanding and, while we were there, put the sheep in another pasture. Some years when grass was scarce, the family who hired the hut before us erected a fence, using posts and chicken wire, to give the children a large, clean playing area. Often they left a bag of sweets for our children as well.

Those weeks on the farm have been really happy times, although tiring for the staff. The children developed confidence; they helped to feed and muck out the horses, watched the blacksmith change the horseshoes - sometimes being given an old one and watched the men unload hay from their lorries. They have looked for rabbits - sometimes up in the trees! They played games impossible in a town garden and visited the cattle market in Ashford. One year when a good friend, Dulcie, was with us, we had an evening campfire. While the sausages were sizzling, Dulcie was serving hot soup. It became almost impossible to serve because grasshoppers kept hopping into it. I believe in some countries grasshoppers are eaten, perhaps not in soup! Of course there have been wet years when we have had indoor games and disco's, but we have never returned early.

In recent years the farm has become smaller. There are still some animals but the greenhouses and sheep belong to other people; the huts are the same and the grass still as green. The apples are no longer picked for sale but taste just as good. Many of the trees were lost in the great storm; some have remained lying on their sides and still bear apples. I see a lesson in that!

Lately we have been able to rent a hut on a yearly basis and, now that we have our own transport, we are able to go more often, in smaller groups, throughout the summer months.

Chapter 14
Photograph Album

As I turn the pages of my photograph albums, I see pictures of the many children who have enriched my life:

Lisa, the baby born with no eyes who came for a month while her parents took the rest of their children on holiday. She was nine months old, so contented, she slept in the daytime and played loudly all night. She came again the following year, then from the age of three to five years, she lived with us from Monday to Friday, spending the weekends at home with her family. She continued to play at night and however hard we tried, we were unable to keep her awake during the daytime. Once she had gone to sleep, it was impossible to wake her.

Lyn, a four year old child with autism, came while her parents visited relatives abroad. She could walk and feed herself but did not seem to understand very much of what we said and did not respond to her own name.

But she could sing very tunefully, especially at four in the morning! Whilst with us she learnt to take off her shoes, socks and knickers, and to put them on again, all in just two weeks. Also we were able to teach her to come when she was called by giving her a reward each time. Her parents were so pleased with her progress when they returned.

Roger, a four year old boy with Hydrocephalus who had a shunt in his head for drainage. He was partially paralysed and had epilepsy. He often vomited and would scream until put to bed. The answer sounded easy - just put him to bed. But if we were out for the day, or shopping, or walking along the sea-front, what then?

He would scream until able to sleep. After three years Roger moved on to a residential school where we hoped he could receive more help for his severe disabilities.

John, the little two year old who had been so neglected that his hands and feet were frost-bitten and swollen to twice their size. I remember the sick feeling I had when dressing him with his hands and feet so painful. What a joy to see him recovering, filling out and making progress. He stayed with us for two years then was placed with a foster family and was later adopted. I often see him now at school and know that he is happy and loved by his family.

A sudden phone call introduced us to *Robert*, a six year old boy. Had we a vacancy and could we take a severely disabled boy within the next hour? Yes we had, could, and did. Robert was the youngest of five, all being admitted to a children's home. This little fellow was so severely disabled that the director of the home did not feel that his staff had either the knowledge or the resources to cope with him. In fact this was the best thing that could have happened for his physical state; I am not so sure about the impact on his emotional one. He was much loved by his brothers and sisters and had everything done for him, consequently he had no experience of doing anything for himself. His legs were not much good but his top half was fine and his IQ assessed at about 115.

He was not helpless just lacking in experience. He started by saying, "I can't", but as that phrase did not mean anything to me, we exchanged it for, "I'll try", which he did and could. No one had ever been prepared to wait for him before, but with us he had all the time he needed.

Firstly he had to learn to put on and wear his callipers, because without them he could only function at floor level. Next was to walk with both elbow crutches and a rotator. At first we encouraged him to climb the stairs on his hands and knees to strengthen his muscles. When he had mastered the art of moving around on his feet, he was able to go up and down stairs quite safely, using the hand rail. At the same time, he had to learn all the self-help things and had to balance himself while doing them; as he would not always find a chair each time he washed his hands, we did not provide one.

After meals each child in the family has a small job to do; Robert chose to push the trolley into the kitchen and to load the dishwasher. Christopher took it upon himself to be chief crutch-bearer and door opener for Robert. Each week Robert's brothers and sisters came from the children's home to have a meal with us and to play with their brother. After a short time it was evident that he would soon be able to go and live with them. To prepare him, and the staff at the children's home, it was decided that he should visit them each week. He stayed only five months with us. He still needed a little help with his mobility, like getting into the mini-bus, but had mastered all the other things which he needed to do.

We took in *Jane*, a girl with autism, who had been living in a residential school. She had been making some good progress and it was felt that she should be offered a family life while attending the same school on a daily basis. She could speak and repeated everything many times. Previously she had severe tantrums and sometimes had hurt herself quite badly. She was clever with her hands and could imitate well. Her love was to be asked to fold up the washing.

For two years she continued to make very good progress but then, sadly, she began to slip back into her autism. She became remote and started having tantrums again, as severe as before. When upset, she was so strong that she could push the piano. For her own safety, and that of the rest of the family, we had to ask for hospital care for her. I asked, "Why?" What made her leave us again? But there did not seem to be an answer.

Now I see a photograph of a very ample young lady; looking at this picture it is hard to believe that *Beryl* was only twelve years old. She came for two weeks while her parents took her younger brother abroad. We were not surprised at her size as she had an incredible appetite.

The first morning her bed was wet, despite the padding; we were warned so were not disturbed. A bath was run for her but she refused it. As she was twice my size, putting her in it was out of the question, as was dressing her without a bath. Eventually, after much persuasion, she did decide to get in and sat down with such a bump that half of the bath water shot into the air and drenched everything in sight. I dried up the mess and withdrew to get clean clothes for both of us. When I returned she refused to get out of the bath, being quite comfortable where she was. I retired saying that I wanted my breakfast even if she did not. This was too much for her, she left the bath like a bullet from a gun, bringing the remaining water with her. My testing time was over and we had no more bath time problems.

Beryl was so amiable and usually instantly obedient. If we told her to go somewhere, she would go at top speed, taking the quickest route and ploughing through anything and any number of people on the way. If we wanted everyone into the garden, we had to ask her to go first as the other children would have been at risk on the steps. When her family returned it was lovely to see the reunion. The little brother took charge of her and she did whatever he wanted.

For a long time we had *David*, a Jewish boy living with us. After some years his school said that he needed more than they could offer; the next school said that they had not the right structure for him. Eventually, after many phone calls, he was granted a home tutor for two hours each morning; I had to occupy him, alone, for the remainder of the day. One room was turned into a schoolroom and he made very good progress with his teacher, covering six months of maths in six weeks. The teacher could not understand why he was so behind. I bought him a large map which we fixed to the wall. We examined all the household articles to see from which country they came and stuck pins in the map accordingly, keeping a log-book as well. Often I was tempted to buy groceries for their country of origin rather than because I wanted them. We also did bird-watching.

With such a large family, about eleven children then, I found it difficult to give David the time that he required, also he needed the company of others of his own age. A boarding school for Jewish boys was tried but by the first half-term, it was not working. Amongst other things David guillotined a pile of books! From his explanation, it seemed that he was just fascinated by the nice neat slices and would have carried on if he had not been discovered. He took the mini-bus keys from the office and started up the engine; when I asked him why, he said he was coming home.

At this time I re-papered his bedroom and the first night he slept there after it was finished, he tore off the new wall paper. He thought that I had covered up the pictures and things that he had on the walls and was looking for them. Another school was found where he seemed happy. After a couple of terms a report came back saying that he only had the intelligence of a two year old. Sadly, by this time his case was out of my hands and I could do no more, but what a waste when this lad was capable of so much.

Two years running we had a little girl, *Sally*, she was three years old when she first came, completely deaf and with severe cerebral palsy. She was a lovely child with a good sense of humour and always smiling. When she tried to help it was impossible to dress her as she became so stiff in her enthusiasm. I am sure that she was of average intelligence. Before she came the second year she had undergone surgery, several times, to lengthen the muscles in her legs and was able to walk a short distance using a rotator. What a struggle; what determination; what a smile!

More recently, in response to an urgent phone call, I accepted, on the spur of the moment, a nineteen year old young man from a boarding school in Scotland. The school was due to close the following day and he had not found a holiday placement. When places are being urgently sort and time is short, vital pieces of information are not always given. This young man needed a home for one month, and we had a bed. The information seemed in order, however, what was not said were the words hyperactive and incontinent at night. Hyperactivity is one category that I do not take as it usually needs a one to one commitment, or to be one of a very active group doing things in the open air.

Ray, my nineteen year old, arrived very tired after the long journey from Scotland. In the morning we found that he had "posted" everything possible through the fan-light of his bedroom. What a good thing that it was a small window or we may have had the bed in the front garden as well! It had certainly kept him busy for a long time, and even longer picking it all up again. Earlier in the year I had painstakingly made a rockery. On the first day, between meals and going out, he dismantled it and, rock by rock, he threw it next door; then spent the evening bringing it back!

He had no speech but he could communicate very well. He told me by signs that he liked to run. That seemed a good way of getting rid of some of his energy. I was on my way to the Post Office so we set off together. He was a great sport and jogged along at my pace, with a smirk on his face, just humouring this old girl who had never done any running before. I came back on my knees, and he was as fresh as a daisy. As we arrived home we met Mr Baker who remarked, "What you need is the bike." That proved to be a wonderful idea; twice every day my young man ran and I rode.

When we went on holiday to the farm Ray loaded and unloaded the suitcases with enjoyment. That was one year when I did not start the holiday exhausted. He ran round and round the orchard, climbed the trees and was in his element. I remember Ray with affection, realizing that I almost bit off more than I could chew. Later I heard that he had been helping to build a road in his school grounds. Perhaps that explained the rockery!

Over the years we have had many workers and volunteers from Switzerland and France. The earlier volunteers came by recommendation of the family I had stayed with while working in Geneva. Many of those since have come through the Evangelical Church at Previssan, near the Jura mountains on the border with Switzerland.

The early days of each young persons stay were difficult. Even when their English was good, lack of practice and a small vocabulary had to be overcome. There is nothing like family living for encouragement, and good progress was made by all. Most of our extended family enjoyed their stay; I was able to take some of them to London for a day's sightseeing.

Over the years we had only three young men. One, *Michel*, stayed while courting his fiancee in Buckinghamshire. One day he was asked to deliver some wood to an elderly lady. This he did gladly but, after he had departed in his Citroen, I was surprised to find the doors and seats of his car left in the front drive. He charmed Christopher with his piano playing. Later, when on his way to his wedding, he came to spend a night with us on the farm. Christopher became very excited as he thought that Michel and the piano were one. This conjured up a lovely image of his Citroen towing the piano!

The second young man, *George*, visited us during the summer holidays. He was quite domesticated but mostly looked after the garden. When we went to the farm he helped us to settle in and to pack up again. He also helped us at week-ends, bringing us vegetables from the garden. We have a lovely photograph of him sleeping in the orchard next to a goat.

The third one, *Jean-Robert*, was given the job of painting the garden fence of white palings about eighty foot long. It was the year in which we were plagued with green fly, blackfly and ladybirds. He would paint a good section, stand back to admire his handiwork, only to discover it was no longer white. To his great discomfort these flies were even on the beach.

Most of our French friends are now married and many have families of their own.

CHAPTER 15
A WEDDING IN SWEDEN

One of our French staff left us to marry a Swede whom she had met whilst working on a kibbutz in Israel. On arriving in Goteborg she was refused entry and was detained in prison for the night. Her husband-to-be secured her release the following day.

We had an invitation to Eliane and Bert's wedding. The fares for Joanne and David were paid for as an educational trip. Our wedding present to the couple was a crocheted double blanket which Joanne carried all the way. David had a small backpack containing all the "smalls", as he could not take it off without help, I knew it would be safe. I had a manageable suitcase mostly containing wedding clothes. I kept hold of David whenever it was crowded. Every time I turned to see where Joanne was, she was right behind me. Even in the most difficult places she managed to follow.

We left at the end of August for eight days. The journey by coach to Victoria then changing for Harwich, took until six o'clock in the evening. The boat sailed at eight o'clock. I do not think it was one of the largest boats, but the children were very impressed. We had a meal, looked around the ship, found our cabin, then it was time to turn in. The night was hot and noisy, we seemed to be next to the engines, none of us slept very well. Next morning we were in good form. There was quite a swell and it was impossible to walk a straight course. This amused the children who spent some time gaining their "sea-legs". Until about ten o'clock we had the ship almost to ourselves. Either the other passengers had a late night or were suffering from seasickness; perhaps a combination of both!

I had not thought of bringing food for the journey, apart from the packed lunch which we had eaten on the coach. Even if I had thought of it, carrying any more would have presented a problem. The food on board was costly but eating took up some time. We had our dinner, saw what the ship had to offer, then looked at the available magazines. There was nothing to see out of the portholes except angry, grey sea. The decks were closed, so what to do for the next eight hours? We played "I-spy", noughts and crosses and a card game which we had brought with us. There was an "Abba" film showing in the cinema. It was very expensive so the children went in while I sat outside, it seemed very short for the price. We had a late tea then gathered our things together. By this time we were approaching land and there was something to see outside. If this was sea travel, I would never be going on a cruise!

At 8 pm we were in Goteborg. I had asked about a room for the night but was assured that there was no need to book as there was always room in Goteborg. Well that night there was not a room anywhere that I tried. Eventually I found a ladies and children's waiting room. The children lay down on the seats and were soon asleep, even though the seats were wooden slats. At midnight a policeman with an Alsatian dog arrived, he said something and began to shout. Of course I could not understand a word of what he said, but it was obvious that I could not stay there. I was trying to hurry the children into their jackets and shoes, the shouting continued and the dog began to bark. The children were confused and frightened. The light was switched off, leaving me groping for Joanne's glasses and trying to remember how many pieces of luggage we had with us. What a commotion! We were hustled out onto the station and the waiting room door was locked.

The station was cold but full of people, many sleeping on the ground in their sleeping bags. I found some seats and the children slept again with their heads in my lap. Joanne stirred once and raised her head, I said something like, "You poor tired girl", "No," she said with a smile and went back to sleep.

Our train for Jonkoping left at 4 am. We found it in good time. The children fell asleep again straight away. A man came and punched the tickets and said something that I did not understand. Anyway, I was past caring and fell asleep. It must have been about two hours later when I was being shaken awake. By the time I had fully come to my senses, the three of us were on the platform, surrounded by our luggage, and the train was disappearing into the distance.

We sorted ourselves out and looked around. It was not Jonkoping and neither was it the time of our arrival. To my relief I found an English speaking station man who said that our train would be along in a short time. I was really thankful that the ticket man on the other train had remembered us, he must have been telling me to change trains. By now we were wide awake and able to enjoy the final part of our journey. What a relief to see our friends on the platform to meet us.

Our friends lived in the country, but, as transport was going to be difficult, had arranged a caravan. It was parked in the grounds of a church in Jonkoping and was more central for us. After a while our friends left us to settle in. I had to go shopping. What a blessing supermarkets are for foreigners. At the check-out I understood nothing and had to trust the girl. September in Sweden was as cold as December at home and for most of the time we wore nearly all of the clothes which we had with us.

I found that there were several places of interest within walking distance. The Tourist Information Bureau directed me to the Bus Station as I wanted to take the children to an island in the middle of a lake. The island was inhabited but the only form of transport there was horse and cart or bicycles. In the bus station I was given a piece of paper with a list of times on it, but no locations or destinations. I could make neither head nor tail of it. Reluctantly I went back to the Information Bureau. The man there spoke English very well; he became quite a friend during our week's stay. He looked at the paper and was no wiser than me; he rang the bus office and discovered that, for all journeys outside the town, the bus left at 9 am and 12 pm and returned at 3 and 6 pm.

One morning, at 9 am, we found the bus for the island of Visinso. It was quite a long journey to the ferry. Each time we came to a hamlet or village where there was no one to get off, the bus hardly slowed down but the doors were opened and the driver threw out a bundle of newspapers. The children thought this great fun and began to anticipate when the next bundle would fly through the air. Although the day had dawned cold and grey, it was now warm and sunny.

I think the ferry might have been the type that was wound by hand along a steel cable. The ride was short but enjoyable. There were several other passengers on the ferry. At the quay they took bicycles from a shed and disappeared. There was no one in sight so we waited. The children said they were hungry so we had our packed lunch. Still no sign of anyone let alone a horse and cart. We walked first one way and then the other, not daring to go too far in case the transport came whilst we were gone. At last it arrived. The cart was very pretty and we sat up high, sideways along its length. We were taken for a long ride to a tower and saw some of the island, arriving back at the quay in time to take the ferry back to catch the bus. On the return journey the driver stopped the bus at every letter box to collect the post.

Our caravan was heated by bottled gas. On our return from the island, I cooked the tea and shortly afterwards the gas ran out. Soon it was too cold to sit in the caravan. Fortunately I had the key to the church as we got our water and used the toilet facilities there. The church had a comfortable room which seemed to be permanently heated so we spent the evening and the next morning there. In the morning I was unable to prepare anything hot so it was comforting to have somewhere warm to sit. During the morning a lady from the Swedish Society for Mentally Handicapped People was coming to meet us. When she arrived I was able to ask her advice about the gas. Her English was very good and she said that her husband would deal with it when he had finished his work.

First the lady took us to see their Club Rooms. They were very pleasant and I think she was proud of them. Afterwards we went to her home for lunch. She had a son with Down's Syndrome who was at a centre, so we did not see him. For lunch we had an assortment of Danish pastries which delighted the children, both having a very sweet tooth. Whilst in Sweden I formed the impression that people there ate a lot of sweet things. The bread was sweet, in fact it was difficult to find unsweetened bread. Sweet bread and hard boiled eggs really do not go together. We had a most enjoyable day, and the lady's husband dealt with the gas. How grateful I was to these two people for their hospitality.

During our stay in Jonkoping it was the wettest time for forty years. At one point there was so much water around the caravan that I thought we might float.

Two children of about ten years old came to visit on several occasions, they must have been very curious about us. We entertained them with drinks and biscuits; our only means of communication were smiles. Bert's parents visited us on two occasions; they were very friendly. On their second visit they brought a present for each of us. The children were each given a china bird and my gift was a blue and white plate with a picture of Habo Church, where the marriage would take place. We drank tea, smiled a lot and did some hand waving, but had no other way to communicate.

The day of the wedding dawned bright and beautiful. This was a real blessing as, with the peculiar bus service, we were obliged to leave Jonkoping at mid-day, arriving at Habo Church a long time before the wedding was due to begin. The steeple of the church stood on the ground beside it. The countryside around was lovely. My aim was to keep the children clean, so we walked and enjoyed the sunshine.

After a long time the guests began to arrive; many of the youths wore national costumes. It seems that each county has its own costume. The church was decorated with small silver birch trees, making an arch over the doorway outside the church, and inside where the couple were to stand.

With Thanks

From the Album

With Thanks

In the garden

There were hymns sung in French and English as well as in Swedish. The service was written out in English for us. The youth group sang many songs in all three languages. The bride looked beautiful in the dress that I had helped her to make, while she was in England. t was a lovely service, full of colour and joy, and is one of my very treasured memories.

We were taken to the reception by car. Everything was arranged so well. The bride and groom sat under another arch of silver birch trees and the tables were beautifully laid out. The wedding cake was unlike an English cake but was very pretty. The atmosphere was very relaxed and, although we did not understand everything, I could talk to the three French folk who were there. The speeches were translated into both French and English. Such a great effort was made to help us to feel the warm welcome we received and we were so happy to be there. But alas, all good things on earth come to an end and, before 6 pm, we had to take our bus back to Jonkoping. We said, "Goodbye", to the happy couple and departed. There was so much to remember and talk about.

Our eight days in Sweden were nearly at an end. Once more we went to see our friend at the information bureau to confirm the times of the trains and to see if and where we had to change. Also I wanted to book a room for our overnight stay in Goteborg, not wishing to spend a second night at the station.

The return journey went without problems and we booked into our hotel room in mid afternoon. We then set out to look at Goteborg and to buy enough food for the journey home. Joanne no longer carried the wedding present so her hands were free to help. Following a meal, we had an early night ready for a prompt start the next day.

During our travels we had collected bus tickets, post-cards and tourist information. I had also stowed away two small drawing books and some paste with an easy applicator. The boat was very crowded and it was impossible to move around. The sea was calm and there were not so many people indisposed as on the outward journey. The same film was being shown so I found a corner with a table and we set about making a scrap-book of our travels. Everything was fresh in the children's minds and, as we had nothing else to do, we relived our eight days by writing and sticking.

The time passed quite quickly but my heart goes out to parents who are frequently on the move by boat because, after the initial excitement, there is not much to do, unless you have a lot of baggage. We were limited because there were not many pencil and paper games that the children were able to play, and neither one of them liked colouring.

The journey went well and we arrived back in England to bright sunshine, from a rather wet and chilly Sweden. I look back on this trip and know that the children benefited from, and enjoyed the experience. The good times far outweighed the difficulties and I would not have missed it for anything.

Another, later announcement of wedding sent a thrill through the family. Christine, who had worked for us for eighteen months, was going to marry Steve. The wedding would take place at the Queen's Road Baptist Church.

As Christine was French, I offered to accommodate her French guests. About six would be staying overnight, with several more during the day. Most of the visitors were already known to us, the young people were pleased to share bedrooms and make room for them. It was all very exciting.

The wedding went off very well. The bride looked lovely if a little chilly. An English wedding with a French flavour that was enjoyed by all. Apparently French weddings last all night, but, true to English form, the celebrations finished in the evening and we returned home. It was good to spend time talking and getting to know some of our friends better.

All too soon we were saying goodbye, it was a pity they could not stay longer, but we promised to meet again. Laurette, Christine's mother, often comes to England now and we have spent some pleasant days together.

CHAPTER 16

EXTENDED ACCOMMODATION AND EXTENDED FAMILY

At one time we had a young woman, Daisy, living and working in the house, she was neither resident nor staff. She was limited in what she could do, mainly because of the restricted life she had led. She was not particularly suited to living within the group and it caused problems. I felt that the best way to deal with it would be to provide her with separate living accommodation, where she would be able to learn and practise her skills. She learnt well and was happy in the flat. She then met someone she was attracted to, married and moved on.

The Shoreditch Tabernacle at Bethnal Green had given us the money to fit out this flat and the experience with Daisy made me realise that there was a need for this sort of teaching. The flat was soon occupied by another quite capable young lady. After much effort we found her some other accommodation to move into and she continued to manage very well.

Next Lucy, a handicapped person, moved into the flat; she too managed very well. The problem was to find ongoing accommodation. One night I awoke with the sure conviction that I must buy a second house. This did not seem pressing and nearly a year passed before I felt the need to pursue the subject again.

I looked around and viewed a number of properties. The ones large enough were too expensive. There were several that could have been altered to fit the purpose but none really appealed to me. I went on holiday and, when I returned, a house in Osborne Road, Broadstairs, was offered. It was a little more than I could afford but I decided to go and see it.

I knew the house as my friend, Connie, lived next door. It was the garden that concerned me. I could hardly manage the one that I had, and I knew this house had quite a large back garden. Never mind, perhaps Syd, Connie's husband, would like some extra work to do! I viewed each room and straight away could see the potential. It was not until I arrived on the top floor that I looked out of the window. The back garden was completely paved over. I could not believe my eyes, even that had been arranged.

My offer for the house was refused. I could not increase it as that was the limit of my bank loan. I could not understand, the house was right, the garden already dealt with, but it was not to be. The Lord must have somewhere else in mind. There was no rush, I could wait. For two or three weeks nothing happened, no more houses were offered. Then the estate agent rang to say that the vendor would accept my offer if I was still interested, so I went ahead.

A lot of work needed to be done before the house would be ready for my young people and, once again, there was the problem of finance. Connie suggested taking students for a year and offered to keep an eye on them. It was a rush to get the place ready for the new term and Syd, Connie and I worked very hard to make it presentable. Although we never had many students in that first year, the expenses were covered.

The alterations went exceedingly slow, mainly through lack of money. Over two years passed before the middle floor was ready for occupation and Lucy moved in. Although this young lady was quite able to manage on her own, a member of staff agreed to move there as well. A year later a second handicapped person moved from the teaching flat at Lynton House to Osborne Road.

During the six years since buying the house, there have been many minor panics, mostly sorted out by Connie, next door. For three years we have used the ground floor as staff accommodation and, apart from the cost of alterations, the house has paid its way.

At the time of writing, a member of staff is poised to occupy the top floor flat as soon as the workman leave and the ground floor is empty for the work to begin there. The young lady in our teaching flat is making good progress and will move there when the work is completed.

Although headway has been slow, I am not discouraged. I feel that the venture is a good one and that God is there. Without Syd and Connie this project could never have come so far. But for Ralph, their Down's Syndrome son, they might never have been interested in, or wanted, people with learning difficulties living next door to them.

In 1973 there were several changes with the family increasing its number. Susan aged fifteen years, Paul five years, Sarah eighteen months and Melony one year, all joined us. What a busy time, as we had already had several changes in the early spring. By Christmas we had eleven children in all, six being under school age. I had four very good helpers. Mum was becoming less able physically but was a very good "pair of eyes" and enjoyed the company of the children and being in the centre of things.

With Thanks

On holiday in France

With Thanks

In the kitchen

Susan is one of twins but not at all like her sister. She had left a boarding school but was unable to adjust to life at home with her mother. During the day she attended the Adult Education Centre, which was just down the road from us. Being used to community life, Susan soon settled down. I think she enjoyed being the eldest. She has always taken a very active part in family life and likes to help. She can read well, likes shopping, has learned to play the recorder with the help of her music therapist and has generally made good progress over the years.

Until recently Susan has been occupied at the adult education centre. When the centre moved to a new building in Margate, she was able to make the journey morning and evening by public transport. In the early days she often came home in tears, having been insulted by name calling and clashes with her fellows at the centre. These have lessened over the years, perhaps she is learning to see trouble coming and avoid it.

During her teens and early twenties she was a member of the Girl's Brigade at Queen's Road Baptist Church. She enjoyed the activities and the company of the other girls. Whilst in the Girl's Brigade she accepted Jesus. Some years later she asked for Baptism, publicly acknowledging Christ as her Saviour. It was a very emotional experience for her and a day we will all remember. She is now a member of the Church.

Susan has a caring family. She is able to visit her relatives each month, making the journey by train. Although she is very involved with them, she regards Lynton House as her home.

In 1989 Susan started work on a cooking project at St Peter's House. She helps to cook for "Meals on Wheels" and for a small restaurant. At first she found it tiring but now has got used to being on her feet all day and really enjoys working.

Paul came looking more like a baby than a five year old boy, with long, blonde, curly hair. He could walk but mostly just stood. He did not seem to understand the spoken word at all. His tantrums, with piercing screams, filled most of our days sometimes as many as thirty a day. Most of the time we did not know what triggered-off the attacks. Cuddling and talking were tried but did not help. It was impossible for the family to live with so much noise, so Paul would be removed to the cloak-room. He always seemed to need a few moments alone before he could stop, then we could take him by the hand and bring him back.

Fortunately, at that time, we had no neighbours, only woodland, next door. Very often he arrived home from school screaming, and had been doing so for an hour before we fetched him. It was very distressing for him and for us. With the same constant handling, the tantrums gradually grew less, but continued at school for a long time after they ceased at home. It took many years before the screaming stopped completely.

I felt that if I could get Paul to understand one phrase, it might just be the key to his understanding of the spoken word. I chose the phrase, "Shut the door", and worked with him many times each day saying it and closing the door. It took about three months before he hesitatingly did it. At last he had achieved something and was very pleased with himself. After that he learned more quickly.

One strange thing he did was always to stand at the hinge side of the door, the handle meant nothing to him. Even when he could understand us, it was many years before he would do the simplest thing without being told stage by stage.

Paul is now a tall, attractive young man, no longer blonde but with dark, straight hair. He cannot speak; he uses a communicator and the Makaton sign language. Although Paul can communicate with us, sadly, we do not always understand what he is saying and he does not always understand us. He stills gets frustrated from time to time and will go off for a walk on his own. Most times he comes back by himself, but occasionally the police, or someone who recognizes him, will bring him home.

Paul keeps in touch with his sister but, owing to the distance involved, we see her only twice a year. He is quite an able young man, when he wants to be, and is attending a course at the Thanet Technical College, but it is difficult to see what the future holds for him.

Sarah was born a twin but her sister died soon after birth. During her first year she lived in a Baby's nursery near London, and that is where I first met her. She was of average size for her age, with almost no hair and her skin was dry and scaly. She could walk holding onto the furniture and had a solemn, determined expression. This determination was to remain with her, helping her to get where she is today. Between her solemn moments she was full of fun and was loved by the staff at the nursery. As she had Down's Syndrome and "could not understand", she was allowed to do whatever she wanted without restraint; her misdemeanours were considered funny!

At eighteen months she was a rascal and was intent only on disrupting and destroying everything. The play-pen came in useful. As she was able to understand actions better than words, she soon realised that her wrong doings were greeted by a spell in the play-pen. Sarah never cried.

One day I noticed that the children around the table were constantly on the move, I wondered why they were so restless. I investigated and found Sarah under the table, pinging the elastic in the girls socks and biting the boys knees.

Sarah could walk around the furniture when she came to us but, despite an operation to both legs and feet, her talipes (club feet) were far from healed. At night she wore boots attached to a bar to position her feet. Over the next four years Sarah underwent two more operations. These were very painful but Sarah showed so much courage for such a little girl. Both her legs were put in plaster from thighs to toes. I borrowed a large, old-fashioned pram and brought her home as soon as the plaster was dry. She did not cry but would gasp with pain when I had to move her.

It was impossible for her to use the potty owing to the height of the plaster which soon became smelly. We were all relieved when, after three weeks, she could go back for the plaster to be changed. She came back from her anaesthetic with the most delicate pair of knee length plaster boots. Knowing my child I asked about her moving around in them. I was assured that she would not but if she did, it would not matter. Within two days we were back; she had stamped the bottoms out and needed a much heavier type.

On another occasion she rubbed a blister on her heel under the plaster. The first we knew about it was the terrible odour, which took us some time to trace. We returned to the Children's Ward at the Royal Sea Bathing Hospital, Margate, and a little window was cut into the plaster so that the wound could be dressed.

Sarah wore callipers until she was about eleven years old. These never seemed to worry her and she did not complain. Callipers, braces and wheelchairs were the normal thing at the Foreland School. The callipers never stopped her playing. On long walks she had to use a buggy for some years.

At Foreland School, Sarah's teacher decided that it was time for her to start to deliver messages and dispatched her to the secretary's office. The secretary called, "Come in" to Sarah's knock but nothing happened, she called, "come in" again and still no one entered. When she opened the door Sarah read her the notice on the outside which said, "knock and wait". Previously there had been a discussion as to whether Sarah understood what she was reading!

From Foreland School, which is for children with severe learning difficulties and where the staff had helped her to develop so well, through some difficult phases, Sarah moved on to St Anthony's School, Margate, a school for pupils with less severe problems. On leaving school Sarah has also been able to attend courses at Thanet Technical College.

Sarah has been a very interesting child. With her love of books, she enjoyed all her school days. Some of the books she chooses appear too complicated for her, but she returns to the same ones again and again. She has had, and indeed still has, an imaginary world in which she often plays. At one point I was worried about her safety when she was out, as she seemed so engrossed in her imagination. She is busily emerging from a child to a young adult. She fusses with her hair and tells others how to behave but at the same time still loves a rough and tumble.

Melony was born at the same hospital as Sarah. Having severe heart disease she remained in hospital for some months, after which she went to live at the same baby's nursery.

I had been asked to take Melony at birth, before the extent of her heart disease was known. Owing to her frailty it was thought that she would not need a long term home. It was some months later, when I was enquiring about Melony, that Sarah was presented to me. Melony was still clinging to life but no long term plans were thought necessary. Six months later I felt sure that she should come and live with us. After many discussions it was decided that perhaps a move from London to the coast might be of some benefit.

Melony arrived aged fourteen months and weighing only fourteen pounds, even though her birth weight had been seven pounds. Not many days after her arrival she developed pneumonia; everyone who saw her thought that her survival was unlikely. It seemed strange to Mum and I that if the Lord had intended to take her, why had he allowed her to come to us? This seemed unreasonable and unthinkable and we prayed wholeheartedly for her recovery, believing that she would be well. Slowly she recovered and has never been really ill since, despite her severe heart defect.

Melony remained very small but she became stronger, walking at about four years. She became an accomplice in crime with Sarah, working on the principle that two could make a much better mess than one.

By the time Melony was two years old, we had four little ones of nursery age, all attending another of Dr. Ludlow's Playgroups. This one was held at St Stephen's Church Hall, Cliftonville. They did the usual playgroup things, helped by willing volunteers. This certainly prepared them for school. Melony was the only one who showed any timidity.

At five years of age Melony started at Stone Bay School. As she tired very quickly the doctor decided that, for the first term, half a day would be enough. She had to travel both ways in her push-chair. As she was still a little clinging, we took her into school the term before from time to time, staying with her for short spells, and so had no problems when her year began.

Melony is basically very shy but unfortunately it comes over in an aggressive sounding voice. If people can get beyond her shyness they will find a loving, caring, funny, helpful person. Small animals are one of her loves, the cat and dog are smothered until they say, "No more", sometimes they have to be rescued, but on the whole they thoroughly enjoy her attentions.

When asked what she would like for a present, it is nearly always pens, pencils and books to colour, at which she spends hours. Melony is not at all academic, unlike Sarah. She saw no reason to learn to read until she was eighteen, when she wanted to read her bible. She had decided and so it worked; very slowly her reading is getting better. However she has a good measure of common sense and is practical. She really likes to work around the house, especially with food, as eating is her passion.

When she was eighteen, she had some tests to see if there was any possibility of helping to relieve her heart condition, as it has progressively affected her life during the last few years. After the tests I was told that there was no treatment and that things would have to take their course.

If you ask Melony how she is, she will brightly say, "I'm fine". We pray God will continue to work in her life. When she was little, she was only given a year or two to live. In some ways she seems to be growing up, in others she is still very much a little girl.

All the way through Sarah's early years she was on the verge of adoption. Each time it fell through. On every occasion it became harder to think of her leaving us. The years sped by and we became more attached.

At one meeting, in an emotional moment after yet another breakdown, I said, "If I could adopt her I would, to be finished with all this uncertainty." There was a silence and then the Social Worker said, "Well you can." I said that financially it was impossible as I had no means of supporting an adopted child and that if I adopted Sarah, I would want to adopt Melony as well, as both had no interested family.

Just at that time plans were being made to pay an adoption allowance for children with handicaps, to increase their chances of having a family life.

There was so much to do before the adoption could take place that it took all of two years. My mother and father had always been their grandparents in name, now they would have an Aunt, an Uncle, and Cousins. I had always been called auntie Jeanne by everyone, but on the day of the adoption they called me "Mum". I thought that in a few days they would forget, but not so. I was no spring chicken and felt really blessed to have not one, but two daughters.

Chapter 17
Time Out

For more than fifteen years I did not take a holiday without the children and had almost no completely free days. I was a mother and that did not seem unreasonable to me. I was full of energy and revelled in good health. There was no spare money, but God had always provided for all our needs. I have never been a person to want material things. As a war child I suppose I learned to value what I had and mum had given us so many pleasures which she created out of next to nothing.

I began to feel constantly tired, I got up in the morning completely exhausted. I kept forgetting things, like the children's appointments; my helpers would remind me but I would forget again. I never seemed to be where I was supposed to be. I had always had a good memory and seriously began to wonder if I was going mad. I did not dare tell anyone. Mum was not well enough and I really thought that someone else might agree. If I tried to find a number in the telephone directory I would get into a panic and dissolve into tears. This was helped a little by a pair of glasses, but, like my memory, my eyes had always been very good. Another worry - was I losing my sight as well? (Bad eyesight ran in my family.)

People standing behind me would send me into a panic, irrational but very real. I slept less and less. When I did sleep it was to have terrible nightmares, some of which occurred over and over again. One particular one was of a car running over a cat outside. I would go with my spade to clear it away and it turned into a baby. This all upset me dreadfully. I became even more convinced that I was going mad.

My helper Helen said that she thought I might be going through the menopause. She said her mother had suffered some of my symptoms some years before and had a small book about it. I had heard that there was a change as one got older but as I read very little, I had not come across any significant information. Helen brought me the book and after reading it I felt a bit better. I was obviously not going mad, my symptoms were quite normal. For a while I calmed down and laughed some of the problems away. But I was totally exhausted and really needed a holiday although I would have been the last to agree.

Eventually I visited my doctor. He was very sympathetic and put me on hormone replacement therapy and agreed that I needed a holiday. I was too tired to cope any more, distressed that Christopher might have to go into hospital care, but knowing now that a separation was inevitable.

The local social worker was contacted; she came straight away. There were eight children and, of course, they each had their own social worker but it was all dealt with for me. In two weeks the children had places, even Christopher, and the packing was done. It was the middle of October. We made the Christmas Pudding and parted with the promise that we would all be home in time to eat it together.

Helen would come in part-time to do some cleaning and to water the house plants. Dad and Mr Baker would look after themselves and Mum would go to my sister's. The house was empty, it was like a bereavement to be without the children, I would be anywhere but there.

My other helper, Erica, a young French girl, who had been so patient and understanding during the year that she had already spent with us, suggested that I should go home with her to France. We travelled by train to Geneva. The journey took about twenty hours, there was no TVG in those days. I am very confused about the first part of that holiday. My first impressions were of a really warm welcome and of a smell of wood burning.

I came to the conclusion that the French were always arguing. I had a few words of French from my earlier year in Switzerland, but not enough to follow the rapid exchanges at meal times. It was several years before I could really follow these family discussions.

That visit lasted eight weeks. I received enough news from the children to keep me happy. I walked in the mountains, pressed leaves and wrote to each child every week. I began to sleep better and although I still had nightmares, they worried me less. I still panicked over silly things. If anyone made me jump, I had the sensation of falling from a great height. Slowly I began to feel rested and a peace came over me; by the seventh week I was looking forward to going home, wondering a little if I would be able to cope.

It was my birthday just before we returned. We had a luncheon and invited friends. Helene, Erica's mother, made a special seafood dish. There were four courses and lunch went on until teatime. Everyone made such a fuss of me.

We travelled back on a night when the temperature was -13°C. I wore my anorak under my coat whilst we waited at Lausanne for our train connection.

The house was opened up. Christopher, Melony and Sarah had to be fetched from London. It was an emotional reunion. All the girls flung themselves at me and cried, the separation had been hard for all of us. I realized that I would have to go away from them again to prepare them for a time when we would not be together. Oh how good it was to be home again, and just before Christmas too!

I feel that it is a pity that the problems of the menopause are not more widely discussed in England. At no time was the subject ever mentioned to me. I thought it was something that came with old age, and at forty-eight I did not consider myself as anything other than young. I had suffered a great deal of mental anguish through sheer ignorance.

Perhaps it was only the severity of the situation that made me take that first holiday, which I needed so badly. I had made many new friends. Erica stood by me through it all with great patience and I had an invitation to visit her home again for a holiday with Helene and Roby.

Erica stayed and worked with us for six years; we had good and bad times. For the children she was a member of the family. When she decided to return to France to get her diploma, I knew it was the best thing for her to do, but the gap she left was so great that it was many months before we got over her departure. For her too, it was hard to leave the family behind.

God is with us in whatever we do, he fills the gaps and heals the wounds, or we could not continue.

Chapter 18
Bereavements

As I have mentioned earlier, my parents and my uncle's brother, Mr Baker, lived with us. The years passed and age crept on. My mother was a severe arthritic with Parkinson's Disease for about twelve years. One by one she gave up her painting and other handicrafts. We found new things for her to do but eventually there was nothing left to try. Even in this condition she talked to her friends about the Lord Jesus. She was an invalid for about nine years, the staff and children helped me to nurse her. Joanne took on the role of personal nurse to Granma, she spent years being so patient and kind to her.

Here I would like to record my gratitude to both Joanne and Helen, a member of staff I have already written about, for their constant care of my mother. It was far from easy as she was often in pain and got depressed. There were also the unpleasant things to cope with in nursing an invalid; I was very often not there at the right moment.

My father's eyesight grew very bad and he became frustrated and irrational in his last years and, at times, violent towards Mum and me, like a small boy with tantrums. He was an independent man and had no wish to rely on anyone. His health remained good and until about six months before he died, at the age of eighty-eight, he was able to go out and about on his own. When he could no longer see or bend enough to potter in the garden, his whole world came to an end.

He spent a number of weeks in hospital, where he had tantrums and threw things at the nurses. He was discharged and came home, we thought better. He had been home a week before I was told that he had cancer and was only expected to live for another five weeks.

At first he wandered about during the daytime, he was quite calm but did not really know where he was. At night he called and knocked continuously for attention. The fight had gone out of him and he just needed comfort. He was incontinent and needed his bed changed about five times each night. To change the bed alone became more and more difficult as he could support himself less and less. When he got onto the floor, which he did on several occasions, I had to call the ambulance men to pick him up! They would help me to change him and settle him again. It is at times like this that one realizes what a marvellous invention is the telephone.

Dulcie, who often came in response to our urgent phone calls, was on hand to cover some nights. But there were eight young people to look after and Mum to be nursed as well and it became apparent that we could not continue. Just at this moment God sent me a young lady who was experienced in several fields. She was able to take on the responsibility of coping with Mum and doing the cooking, while I set about looking for a nursing home where Dad would receive the care he needed in his last weeks. I was able to visit him often and, without the responsibility of his care, became closer to him in those last weeks than ever before. He died peacefully on 5th May 1987.

Mr Baker had suffered from angina for a number of years but nevertheless was a very active man and frequently walked to Ramsgate and back. Four or five days after my father's funeral he suffered a slight heart attack and was taken to Margate hospital. He had never been in hospital before and was alarmed by the experience. When I visited him the following day he expressed a wish to come home. I spoke to the sister and was told that he would be home in a couple of days as his attack had been a very mild one. At about 11.30 pm that night I was woken up by the telephone, to be told that Mr Baker had a heart attack and a stroke and had died. I was completely shattered. He had looked well when I saw him that afternoon, the fact that he might die had not crossed my mind.

This friend, my friend for about fifteen years was gone; I had not even been able to say goodbye. I do not know if he was a committed Christian. I do know that he loved the family at Lynton House and had done all he could to ease my load. He took on the role of grandfather, even though he was not married, taking the children to school and mending things that came apart. He took time to teach and work with Paul. I was able to talk confidently to him about financial matters, he would listen and advise if he could. He loaned me the money to buy Lynton House and insisted on giving up his work five years early, so that he could move with us and help with the repairs to the home.

Life was difficult after Mr Baker's death. I missed his presence in the house, I missed talking with him. He enjoyed the family outings and parties and would relate the funny things the children did. Now each time there was an annual outing or a birthday this feeling of loss was present. Mr Baker was a gentleman in his ways. He was seventy-six years old when he died.

In just three weeks we had two funerals. Mum coped very well with the first one but had difficulties the second time, and was not well enough to attend.

The children were wonderful. Of course they cried and had to grieve. Even in their sorrow they were so helpful and kind to each other. We were upheld in prayer by so many friends. At times when one is empty and bereft of all feelings, it is good to know that friends are with one in thoughts and prayers.

Chapter 19
Family Life

As the years passed and several of the children had grown into adults, I felt concerned about our Church life. It took a long time, and much prayer, before I decided to seek new pastures. I wanted a Church where the young people could become involved rather than be spectators on the edge of things.

It was a big step, and not an easy one. I took the family to all the churches in the area, most made us feel welcome. I made a list of the pros and cons, out of which emerged some relevant information. If I chose a church outside Broadstairs we would not meet our friends in our daily comings and goings, also the more able members could not get there alone without expense.

I discovered that in Churches with no structure to the service, we did not know when we must be quiet, praise, sit down or stand up. With one or two members in the family this would have been possible, but with ten of us all doing our own thing, it was very noisy and disturbing.

The Queen's Road Baptist Church had been considered from the outset. It was in Broadstairs and we had links through the Girl's Brigade, but I had to be sure that it was right for us. After a number of months being nomads, I made the decision to attend Queen's Road. It was good to be with a permanent Church family again.

We are at home in our Church now and new members of our family have settled in there very quickly. We join in and are part of things. Helping with washing-up and delivering leaflets is well within our scope, we are loved and accepted just as we are. I hope that in the years to come, more of the young people will realize the wonderful truth of the Saviour's love and, as their skills improve, there will be more ways for them to serve.

Our Church life is really important to us. We are slowly getting to know more folk, we need the support of other Christians. As a family, I am sure that we have a lot to offer and, as individuals, have so much love to share.

We hold our own songs of praise each week. The singing is not wonderful, often very off key, but comes from the heart. It is helped along when someone plays for us. The young people are encouraged to take part

and express themselves in prayer. I hold
study for the more able ones each week, but
something that I do not do well.

I started a Hobbies Group many years ago. Local girls with learning difficulties join us for an hour and a half each week on a Tuesday evening. They bring along their handicrafts and we talk, have tea and biscuits, and I read to them from books like "Peep Behind the Scenes"; the Patricia St John books are also very popular. Some very nice tapestry and knitted garments have been made during these sessions. Sometimes in the summer we do our work outside and, to make a change, we have meals together; it is a good way to celebrate birthdays.

The group is well attended and unless the girls are ill, they never miss an evening. They enjoy meeting in this informal way. As most of them are not able to travel alone at night, they have no opportunities to visit friends in the evenings.

I do not aim to teach during these sessions, but often spend the time picking up dropped stitches and threading needles. It is a happy evening each week, if it was not successful the girls would not continue coming.

For many years now I have had the privilege and pleasure of spending my holidays with Helene and Roby in France, I have been able to watch the children, of those who have worked in Lynton House, grow up. Over the years my understanding of French has improved, together with the knowledge of how much I do not know and the mistakes I make.

In 1987, the year in which my father and Mr Baker died, I decided to take my two adopted daughters on holiday with me. Although I did not have the rest that perhaps I needed, my mind was bruised from our recent losses, looking after the girls kept my thoughts occupied and I was not able to dwell too much on what was passed.

We were due to leave Gatwick early in the morning, too early for a coach. There was little difference between the return train fares, and the cost of a car there and a coach back. So we made the easy journey to Gatwick by car, booked in early and got rid of the baggage. The girls were interested and excited about everything from the juice machine to the little cars carrying people. Sarah was fascinated by all the different flight numbers and destinations

There was one nasty moment as we went through customs. The Passport Officer asked me for confirmation of the adoption. That was the one thing that I had not thought about. He said that it did not matter to him but that the Swiss authorities would not let us in. I must admit I was a little worried and wondering what would happen when we arrived in Geneva did spoil the flight for me. The girls were unaware that there was a problem and were still bubbling with excitement.

There was a delay of about an hour on the ground, but by the time we had inspected everything in front of us, put the tables up and down a few times, changed places and talked about the things we could see from the window, including the fact that the object sticking out beneath us was a wing, it was time to take off.

As usual Sarah sat back and took it all in her stride. Melony was a little nervous during the take-off but relaxed as soon as we were airborne. She was excited to see that the wing was still attached and insisted on sharing this piece of information with the passengers behind us and every stewardess who passed.

Both girls were delighted when the little lunch-trays were brought round. It was like the best present they had ever had. I rearranged the hand luggage to make room for all the little bits and pieces that we had not used. The stewardess played along and entered into their fun. I think it was the shortest flight ever for me.

Roby and Helene met us at the airport and took us home. The girls were not shy to use the few words of French that they knew. They quickly learned a French grace to sing at meal times, and now when we sing this grace at home, we usually have to follow it with the French version.

The girls enjoyed their first night in Collonge Fort L'ecluse, sharing Erica's bedroom. The following day we went to the Jura mountains to stay in a chalet that had been a farm. It was home from home for me as I had been there a number of times and always enjoyed my visits, but for the girls it was an adventure.

They talked about the film "Heidi" which they had seen and were able to notice the similarities. In spite of the weather, which was not very kind to us, the girls enjoyed themselves. Melony struggled a little when out for a walk but we were never in a hurry and she could make it up the slopes at her own speed. She did complain a little for the terrain was not really very suitable for her.

We had our dinner out on the mountain, cooking sausages on a campfire. It was springtime, everywhere was covered with flowers. We had much pleasure in watching a stoat running backwards and forwards in front of the house.

Every two or three days we went back to Collonge to pick fruit and vegetables and to do the washing. The girls were not too keen on picking strawberries, but they enjoyed eating them - especially with lots of cream. The fruit was taken back to the mountains where we helped to make jam; the girls enjoyed stoning the cherries using a machine. They liked helping Helene in the kitchen; she had so much patience but must have breathed a sigh of relief at the end of our stay.

One day the ladies from the church at Prevessen, with their children, joined us for a picnic. Despite the language difficulties, the girls joined in and we all had a good day. Another day there was a children's fun afternoon at the church, with a film and tea. The girls stayed with one of our au-pair girls. They both enjoyed the afternoon, Melony most liked clearing the tables and washing-up. Helene and I took the opportunity to go shopping.

On arriving in the mountains I had a quick look around the cow-shed, just in case there was anything that might cause trouble. I found nothing to worry me. Although the girls were in their early teens, one can never be too sure of what they might do. One afternoon Helene and Roby went to visit an elderly couple who lived further down the mountain, by the road. Suddenly I was aware of Sarah coughing and retching and Melony complaining that she had drunk it all. All around Sarah's mouth was red and her lips looked slightly burnt. They showed me a small, empty bottle which had a very strong smell. It had a label but with my very limited French, I could not read it. What did I know about poisons? Acid or alkaline? Milk or water? I did not know what the bottle had contained.

I made Sarah rinse out her mouth with water and sat her down with strict instructions not to move. I prayed like I have never prayed before. The car was outside but there was no road. Even when it is dry the way was difficult because of the rocks, and it had been raining for days. If I drove the car and got it stuck in the mud, it might take longer than if I waited for help to come. It seemed imprudent to try. I tried all manner of things to attract attention; I yelled until I had no voice left; I blew on the recorder as loudly as I could; I banged on a saucepan hoping that the mountains would carry the sound. Every few minutes I went indoors to look at Sarah who, apart from her mouth, seemed all right.

After half an hour, I was just beginning to look at the car again when our friends appeared over the rise. With a quick explanation and armed with the offending bottle, we set off for La Roussee hoping to find a doctor. The journey down seemed very slow, it must have taken about 30 minutes. We found a doctor who phoned the

Poison's Bureau. Apparently the liquid was a disinfectant used by the vet, who had called while we were out and left his rubbish behind. The doctor thought that the bottle must have been almost empty, apart from the dregs, and told us to give Sarah only milk for the rest of the day. He appeared quite taken by these two girls with Down's Syndrome and asked me many questions.

What Sarah had done shocked me; in my opinion she would have been the one least likely to do such a thing. The situation could have been more serious. Melony has never let Sarah forget her misdemeanour and brings the subject out for an airing from time to time.

Soon we had to pack for the return journey, which proved to be just as exciting as the outward one. The girls were now veterans and not at all apprehensive! Once again the luggage had to be rearranged to accommodate all those little things that we just had to take home for the family.

There were so many people in that part of France who knew me and we were pleased to meet so many friends. I was really proud of the girls during our stay.

Chapter 20

Joanne and Christopher

Time was passing for Joanne and Christopher, the original two from Dover. During childhood, Joanne had suffered repeatedly with painful ears, several times having grommets inserted to drain the fluid. This has resulted in a slight hearing loss.

When Joanne was about nine years old, I began to worry about her progress. I went to her classroom on several occasions and each time she was doing the same things that she had been doing three or four years earlier. As mentioned previously, she learnt to read before starting school and was now bored with reading the same early books over and over again, her thirst for reading was slowly dying. I made an appointment with the head-master which got me nowhere. I was told that, "The only thing parents ever wanted was for their children to read and write".

When this is within the capabilities of a handicapped child, I can see only blessings in such an achievement.

With Thanks

At the piano, Lynton House

With Thanks

My family

Even if the reading is limited to recognizing radio and television programmes, the contents of a tin or box, information from Church or around the town: this can give an added measure of independence. To be able to read even short, simple books can bring hours of pleasure.

I talked to the school doctor about my worries, she suggested that perhaps Joanne needed a change of school and said she would look into the matter. All of you will know how slowly the wheels of bureaucracy turn. Several months passed and, by the end of the summer holidays, I had heard nothing. On the first day of term, I arrived with Joanne at the new school, St Anthony's School, Margate. No one had heard of her. I was asked if she had an IQ test recently, to my knowledge she had not. I said that I was sure that this was the school where she should be and after some more debate, she stayed. She was never a brilliant child but she did benefit from being in a more formal school setting with children who were more able. She could look after herself and her property and was a practical young lady.

Joanne progressed through St Anthony's School, having her ups and downs like any child. She had a fascination with rubbers and made great collections of them; as they mostly belonged to other people, we were always returning them. We never solved the problem, it fizzled out when she left school and had no more rubbers to collect.

When she was ten years old, Joanne joined the Girl's Brigade. She enjoyed the meetings; it was the highlight of her life at that time. For some weeks she was taken there by a voluntary escort who lived nearby. One day the escort apologized for not having told me that she had been away the week before. When I asked Joanne about it she said that she had knocked on the door and when no one answered, she went by herself. Previously she had not ventured alone farther than our local shops, and, as it had been dark, I was a little disturbed. But Joanne had used her initiative and once again had proved herself more capable than I had thought.

She moved on from school to the local adult education centre, where she was occupied for nearly nine years. She travelled backwards and forwards on public transport and enjoyed the independence and the company of her friends.

As I have already mentioned, Joanne helped to look after my mother. My mother was getting older and when I realized that it would be hard for Joanne when my mother was no longer there needing her, so I looked around for another outlet for her love. The headmaster and teacher of the Special Care Unit at Foreland School agreed to let Joanne help as a volunteer for two mornings each week. Joanne had always liked babies and children so this was worth trying. She would make the drinks, wash-up and talk with the children. Later she progressed to helping on swimming days and in the dark room. She put her heart into her work, knew all the children and what they could do; she was so sad when they were ill or in hospital.

When Granma died Joanne grieved with the rest of us. She realized that Granma had been in pain, and, being brought up with faith in a living God, she knows that she will meet Granma again one day.

The work at the school was very helpful to her during that sad time. She continued with her little ones until she had the opportunity to join the cooking project.

Just after I adopted Melony and Sarah, Joanne began to shoplift. It was some months before we realized that perhaps the two events were connected. Each time we took the goods back, the shopkeepers involved were very helpful in the way in which they dealt with the matter. It was worrying and embarrassing and we were becoming very suspicious. It took me so long to see what her real need was. One day, while talking with her, she said, "But I need a Mum too." We cried together and I said that I would see what I could do.

On making enquiries I discovered that Joanne could go to a solicitor and change her name by Deed Poll. I wrote to Joanne's mother who has always kept in touch by post, and she was happy with the arrangement. As far as Joanne was concerned it was all in a name, and I became her "Mum". With the change of name she considers herself one of the family and it filled her need. The answer to, "What's in a name?" was EVERYTHING, and, as far as I know, there have been no more problems.

We did have another scare whilst she was helping at Foreland School, when she unlocked the Tuck Shop and took some sweets. When I questioned her about it, she said that the other teachers did it. She considered herself one of the staff and thought she had the right. When I explained, she was happy to pay for what she had taken and the matter was closed.

Joanne likes her work on the cooking project. At first she missed her friends at the Centre, but she sees them each week when she collects her wages and at the Thanet Mencap Gateway Club. She enjoys the club; likes dancing and pop music. Her bedroom is festooned with the latest stars. She is not a talker and has to be encouraged to join in the conversation.

At the age of twenty-five years, she accepted the Lord Jesus as her Saviour and asked for baptism. She was duly accepted into Church membership.

Joanne continues to progress. She continues to care and she continues to hide things belonging to the people she likes best! When she came to me at ten days old, her prognosis was poor. I was told not to love her too much as it would break my heart. The suggestion was that I put her into a long-stay hospital, the only provision in those days. How pleased I am for my stubborn nature, but for that I might have missed these years with Joanne.

We left Christopher when he started school. He first walked at seven years old. Shortly after he was very seriously ill and his survival was doubtful but, after several alarms, he rallied and was soon well enough to come home from hospital.

When a child like Christopher, with so many problems, is at death's door, it is difficult to know how to pray. I knew that God was in control and His will would be done, but my love for this weak, little boy was very deep. I had nursed him through many illnesses, sat up so many nights, had helped him conquer his many fears. Our lives had become bound together. Perhaps the Lord was showing me that He alone was supreme and must take first place in my life.

Christopher had not been very big before his illness and had lost a lot of weight. It was several months before he was able to walk again. That was his last really serious illness although the oxygen cylinder remained in our cupboard for many more years, to be used from time to time.

When I applied for the Mobility Allowance for him my application was turned down. By this time he could walk around the house, but used a wheelchair outside. He would not travel on a bus, despite the many attempts to get him used to it in the early days. He became distressed to the point of exhaustion and would become blue and limp. As he became bigger, he would clutch at the other passengers in his frantic efforts to get off.

When he was small we travelled to Guy's Hospital by train. He would cry all the way, his clothes becoming soaked with perspiration. It was very stressful and as he grew heavier I abandoned that mode of travel as well.

In the early days of the Mobility Allowance there were certain categories for which the allowance was granted. Although Christopher had Down's Syndrome, a severe congenital heart defect, was blind and suffered from epilepsy, none of these conditions alone made him eligible for the allowance. I contacted the local Society for the Mentally Handicapped. The Secretary wrote to the National Society who arranged to take our case to the Appeal Court in London, to appeal on behalf of all children with multiple handicaps. The Appeal Court was on the fourth or fifth floor of the building. Christopher was in very poor shape after the journey and I did not dare to use the lift, so I carried him up all the stairs. By the time we made it, we were both in need of oxygen! The Mobility Allowance was awarded and it opened the way for other children with similar health problems. I did not enjoy the experience but, when it was over, I was pleased to have assisted.

When Christopher was twelve years old, he awoke one morning with a very swollen face. He had an abscess under his back molar and was in considerable pain. Painkillers and penicillin were prescribed. Owing to Christopher's heart condition, the dentist was unable to remove the offending tooth. It was a week before he could be admitted to Canterbury Hospital. He had his four back molars removed so that his wisdom teeth could come through more easily. Christopher did not complain, he just sat around on the floor, with his head propped up on his knees, very still and quiet for several days.

Christopher has regularly visited an eye specialist. When he was twenty-two years old, it was thought that, with laser treatment, he might gain more sight.

In 1988, just before Christmas, we went to the Out-patient's Department of the Kent and Canterbury Hospital. I explained to Christopher what the doctor would do and what he must do, and he was very co-operative. Alas, each time he swallowed, he blinked and he was unable to control his continuous eye movements. The doctor tried for a long time but found it impossible to carry out the treatment, and decided that a further attempt would have to be under general anaesthetic.

In July of the following year, Christopher went into hospital and what I thought was to be laser treatment, turned out to be an operation on both eyes. Christopher took it in his stride and his heart stood up well. One of his eyes clouded over after the operation and now has no sight, but the other one is very good. At first he had to recognize what he was seeing. Although his sight is not perfect, he can now see so much more. He wants to learn to read but, as yet, I am not sure if he can.

The wonderful thing about it all is that his speech has really improved. How he has so much more to talk about and so many new words to use. He has a happy nature and has gained some independence but still needs quite a lot of help in certain areas. His life has been playing the piano which he learnt to do very early on. He now attends the Adult Education Centre where he enjoys playing for the other clients.

When I look at this young man, it is difficult to remember that he was such a fragile baby, always at death's door. We never dared to plan ahead for him as it seemed unlikely that he would stay. I love him and he gives me such joy.

Chapter 21
Peter

In 1986 we had a vacancy as one of our older girls had moved on. I talked with the older members of the family and the staff to see whether they would prefer an adult or a child to join our family. The vote was unanimously for a little one. When I pointed out that babies make a lot of work; that I should expect some help; and that we would not be so free for outings, they still insisted that it should be a young one. We prayed about our empty bed and asked the Lord to send someone to fill it.

Not long after, I received a phone call from social services asking if I would take a severely handicapped little boy within an hour. His name was Peter, he was two and a half years old.

We pulled out the cot, cleaned off several years worth of dust, and put it together. When Peter arrived he was too long for the cot. His mother assured me that he slept in a bed and had never fallen out because he could not move. He was an attractive little boy with fair, wavy hair. He had some angry red patches of eczema around his ears and on his arms and legs. During the first few days he did not move at all and seemed very weak and listless.

Peter would not or could not eat, and had existed on cups of tea and yoghurt for some time. Our efforts to feed him were greeted with screaming, but we did manage to get some food into him. He began to smile and to move his arms and legs and to follow us with his eyes. He became so active that one morning he was not in his bed but underneath it! We barricaded the bed with furniture until Peter's father, who is a carpenter, had made some wooden sides for it. He has solved and filled quite a few of Peter's needs.

At times Peter seemed to get a little better at taking food and would gain some weight, only to lose it again with the next infection. During the good times he was happy and active, during the bad times he was miserable and listless. Both his parents visited him every week and sat with him for a short time.

I reverted to bottle feeding, wondering if I could slowly wean him again. Peter did not object. He chewed on the teat and made contented noises but he was unable to suck, even with an enlarged hole. After a short time I abandoned bottle feeding as useless. Meal times became a battle. Peter would scream to a point of exhaustion, but he also cried bitterly when he was hungry.

By now he was attending the pre-school unit at Foreland School. Chris, a teacher at the school, had some knowledge of children with feeding difficulties and undertook to feed him at lunch-times. He tried everything he knew but had no more success than we had. During all this, Peter made no physical progress and gained no weight, but, in my opinion, his understanding had been developing. He knew when we were pleased or cross and his facial expressions changed accordingly.

One day, in the late afternoon, I told him that his daddy was coming to see him. My helper put him to bed at about 6.30 pm and he cried with big tears rolling down his face. We could not find anything wrong with him. Later his daddy arrived; we had forgotten but not Peter! Since then I have been even more careful to explain to him what I am doing, and the events that will take place.

In the spring of 1989, when Peter was five years old, a new Speech Therapist at school suggested we try the feeding clinic at Great Ormond Street Hospital. We had not heard of it but were pleased to get an appointment for June. Michael, Peter's father, and I took him to the Clinic, armed with his dinner and clean clothes. Trying to feed him was as bad as usual. The doctor thought that Peter's development was so retarded that he was not able to cope with things in his mouth and that his mouth had become hypo-sensitive thus causing him pain. The suggested treatment was either a nasal gastric tube or a gastrotomy (a feeding tube passed through the abdominal wall into the stomach).

I was shocked and horrified by the latter but, as there was no way in which we could continue as we were, perhaps I would be able to cope with the nasal gastric tube. How would we manage? The tube would be put in the first time by our local hospital and we would be taught how to do it.

The journey home was awful. We got stuck in the evening rush-hour traffic and it was incredibly hot. Peter was tired, hot, and hungry. Once on the open road he went to sleep. Michael was shocked and upset. I felt torn between the guilt of having made this child eat against his ability, and the knowledge that if he had not received the food he would have died. Perhaps it would have been better to have let him go, but that is a decision for God alone. It brought me back to the question, why had the Lord given him to us? - he could have died at home.

The nasal tube was put in place at the beginning of July. I watched and we went home with a small machine and boxes of supplies. Peter was to be fed overnight. We had no drip stand but Michael came in response to my phone call and supplied a peg on the wall for the feed, and a metal tube on the head of the bed for the pump. Only having watched the machine being put together once, I was nervous of making a mistake. Sally, a nursing friend from church, came hurrying round and we got it going. She came again the next night to watch me do it and after that I managed. That is until the night it would not drip. I rang the hospital and was given information on what might be wrong but still could not get it working.

I rang Sally but it was Carnival night and she was not at home. My family were all at the carnival and I was at home with Peter and the baby, who had joined us some months before. I called a neighbour who said she would have the baby, and I was about to leave for the hospital with Peter when Sally arrived. She showed me what to do; it is really easy when you know how!

The first time I put the tube down, I took one of my helpers with me to the Children's ward at the local hospital, where I could receive he]p should I need it. As the tube had to be changed at least every ten days, it was absolutely essential that I knew how. The first time was not too difficult, Peter had not learnt how to resist; that came later.

Several weeks later a member of staff came to tell me that Peter had vomited and had the end of the tube coming out of his mouth, while the other was still attached to his nose, and what should she do? I had absolutely no idea! I suggested that she held him up while I rang the hospital yet again. "Oh" said the nurse, "Just pull it out." I was horrified and rang Sally who was not at home, so I rang Dulcie's daughter Judith, who came straight away. Another lesson learned and it was something that we had to do more frequently as the months passed.

We had many problems: Peter stretching in his sleep and pulling the tube out; the connections would come undone; power failures. Some resulted in a pint of milk in the bed, others in an unfed child.

Peter was vulnerable to infection and had several spells in hospital. This enabled me to catch up on my sleep. New staff had to be shown the way of tube feeding; some were upset by it.

By the spring of 1990 it was obvious that all was far from well. Peter resented the tube and rejected it at every opportunity. It became a fight to put it down and eventually we were doing it every day, sometimes twice. Peter was sick repeatedly and weighed no more than a year earlier. He was having less and less food at night and we were obliged to supplement it during the day with high calorie food in a cup. The feeding battle was never ending. We all felt that we spent so much time fighting with feeds that there was no time to play.

When we visited the feeding clinic in June 1990, I was prepared to try the gastrotomy offered. It could not be worse than the nasal tube and just might be better.

Peter and I were admitted to Great Ormond Street Hospital in October. He was in very good health; he had his operation and remained well throughout. Although he lost weight, he had regained it by the time we went home.

At the hospital, the arrangements for parents are very good; most children seem to have someone staying with them. The information and rules are all printed and I received my copy with the notice of admission. I took plenty to do for the times that were not occupied with caring for Peter. I found the small room reserved as a chapel and was pleased to spend some time each day alone in the quiet. I went there every day but never met anyone else.

The hospital was full of bustle and people. As the parent's sitting-room was the only area reserved for smoking, I could not sit there. Many of the nonsmoking parents said the same thing and we stayed in the ward until bedtime.

I shared a bedroom with four other mothers. There were two bunk-beds, the bottom two were already occupied when I arrived. Being just five foot tall, the top bunk was level with my head when I was standing on the floor. There was nothing for it but to climb. What a pantomime! I had to get up onto the bed to make it up, turning round and round as I went. This mountaineering caused many laughs and I became very friendly with the mother sleeping under me. We found ourselves arriving earlier for bed so that we could talk.

Michael visited Peter on Saturday and I took the opportunity to go shopping in Oxford Street, something I had not done for ten years or more. I walked a little each day and on Sunday visited the Bloomsbury Baptist Church.

The nursing staff were friendly and helpful as I learned how to deal with Peter's new requirements. Just one week later, equipped with boxes of supplies to cover the next month, we were discharged. Peter was in top form, he was excited and active; I am sure he knew he was on the way home.

For three days he was very contented and we had no problems with the feed, although the pump we had was not very suitable for Peter's new requirements and a new one would be needed. These three days were followed by the miseries, Peter moaned all day long but we could find nothing wrong. The following day I took him to the dietician to talk about pumps, and, while at the hospital, we saw a doctor in the Children's Ward. He looked at Peter and made a few suggestions but could not see any real reason why he should be so miserable. By the late afternoon he had developed a very red throat and by the next morning he had a fever and his wound was inflamed and oozing. Despite antibiotics the wound was slow to heal.

Our days are still punctuated by feeding Peter but there are no more terrible fights over food. Since his operation he has had a series of infections but on the whole I find him more relaxed and contented. He is gaining weight and generally looks better.

Chapter 22
The Future

In the years leading up to 1985 I became increasingly preoccupied with the question of what would happen to my family when I was no longer able to care for them. This is a subject which fills the minds of all natural parents from time to time.

For many years this problem remained in the background, there did not seem to be an answer. I was young and succeeded in pushing the thought far enough away so that it did not trouble me too much. Eventually I had to face the fact that I could no longer use my youth as an excuse and should address the matter seriously.

I could just sit back and say, "Well, I won't be there, so the problem will not be mine." In fact this will be so whatever I decided. I owed it to my family to make some plans which might make their situation easier and give them security when I died or felt the need to retire.

Here was a house to which many people had contributed over the years. Home for a group of young people, in a neighbourhood where they were known and had their interests. Although most had not managed to make any deep friendships, they all had many acquaintances in the area. I felt that they should at least be given the opportunity to remain in their home if they so wished.

If these young people had been my natural children, at my death, they would have received an inheritance from the sale of the property. It is debatable whether a cash sum or money invested is really of any benefit to people with mental handicaps.

The money that has been spent on the property is rightfully theirs, any that might have been mine I would have given to them with love. As far as I could see, the only way that they could realize their inheritance would be for me to leave the house in trust for them. But in trust with whom?

First I looked around the family, but there was no one with any knowledge of running this type of home. Next I turned my attention to various organizations. I found a few, but none, within the Christian Faith, that really appealed to me.

I talked to people and prayed about the matter with my staff, one of whom, Carol, was awaiting a place at a school of nursing. She lived in Strood. One weekend she came back from home with a pamphlet that she found in her church. She was very excited as it looked like an answer to our prayers.

The pamphlet was written by the Reverend David Potter. It appeared that he had some connection with homes like mine. I wrote and said I was interested in his work and could he send me some more information about "A Cause for Concern".

The information told me that David and Madelaine Potter were parents of a girl with Down's Syndrome. Like me, they had looked around and were not satisfied with what they found and had set out to do something about it. I was impressed with what I read and thought that my next move should be to visit one of the homes that had been opened by "A Cause for Concern".

The nearest home was in Maidstone. This was for three people with Autism. I did not think that this would give me a good view as it would be too specialized. The home in Reading was for sixteen adults and, although in my opinion it was too big, I thought that I should be able to gain a general feel of the place.

Writing for an appointment was difficult as I did not want to make any commitment. I wrote and said I was interested in the work that "A Cause for Concern" was doing and would like to make a visit. The reply was favourable and I was invited to lunch. This visit was not easy for me as I was beginning to focus on a time when I would no longer be involved in Lynton House.

The residents welcomed me and, after lunch, showed me their rooms which were very individualistic. There was a staff change-over meeting to which I was invited. I liked the way problems were discussed and how they were resolved in a sensitive and positive manner.

It appeared that this home in Reading was being run along much the same lines as Lynton House although, at that time, most of my family were still in full time education. "A Cause for Concern" opened their own homes and there was no guarantee that they would consider taking over one that was already running. On returning home I was pleased to share the days events and my feelings with my staff and we thanked the Lord for progress so far.

By this time I had purchased a house in Osborne Road, to convert into flats for independent living. It was in the throes of alteration, with all the chaos that entails. Perhaps that would not help as it was only in its infancy, and I did not yet know if I would be able to get that project off the ground.

Now was the time for me to write again to David Potter, explaining what I had in mind. This time he made an appointment to visit us. It was a short but pleasant occasion. After lunch, and viewing Lynton House, we went to Osborne Road. There we sat amid the mess and committed the work to the Lord in prayer.

David had to go back and talk to his Committee about what I wanted. They agreed to take over the home when I felt the need to retire or if I should die first. This has given me peace, knowing that the work which I started will not die with me and that my family will only have to leave if they want to. I know that they will be secure and loved, whatever they decide.

CHAPTER 23
HOME BECOMES A HOME

At first, when I was away on holiday, my sister looked after my mother in her home. During the last few years of my father's life, she had him there as well. But mum became less and less able, needing so much nursing, that in the end she had to go into a Nursing Home during my breaks.

In the early summer of 1987, I had left her quite well but when I returned she was under the doctor for bronchitis and was not well enough to come home. However she got a little better and, one Sunday, I went to see her with the intention of bringing her home, only to find her in bed again very poorly.

She did not wish to live. She had lived her life, suffered severe pain and was just waiting to die, to be with her Lord and Saviour. Our Minister visited her the following day, she was sleeping and about two hours later, without waking, she died. When she died, just fourteen months after my father, my mother was seventy-nine years old.

She had been very deaf in her last years and we had to make a special effort to see that she knew what was going on. She had used quite a lot of equipment for her disabilities and had a special armchair in every room on the ground floor. Looking after her had taken a large part of somebody's day because, at the end, we could not leave her on her own.

It was many months before we fully adjusted to her absence. I missed her dreadfully, which made me sad but I was truly happy for her because she did not wish to stay any longer

In the September after my mother died, we became aware that when Paul left school the following July, our number of adults would exceed the legal limits. Although I had always been a registered foster mother, my family was growing up fast. As well as the children, I was allowed to have three adults but Paul would be the fourth.

I had two options. The first was that one of the adults would have to leave, but which one? Christopher and Joanne had been with me since their birth; Susan and Paul had arrived at the same time, fourteen years earlier.

I could not make that decision and I did not feel that it was one that I should have to make. The second option, if one could call it that, was to become a Registered Home for Adults.

Although everyone had a room of their own, some of the rooms were not of regulation size. Our central heating system was solid fuel and was not efficient enough to heat every nook and cranny to the required temperature. We had completed the fire precautions to standard sixteen years before, but the requirements had changed and it all needed bringing up to date. In all, as far as I could see, we needed at least £26,000 of which we had £7,000. We could not shilly-shally as time was running out; the day Paul left school was the last one by which we could register.

With prayer and in faith that all would be well, we embarked upon the huge task. The builders were in the house for almost four months; it was difficult working with all the mess. My staff were marvellous and just kept going; cleaning was useless but had to be done. The hardest part for me was seeing my home being transformed into a HOME. The day the door closers went on was truly the most terrible day. I went through moments of great stress during those four months, wondering if it was really worth it and if all my work had been in vain.

The builder did not press us for payment, we paid what we could whenever possible. Our £7,000 was similar to the oil and flour in the story of Elijah, 1 Kings 17, verses 13-15. But, unlike that story, our money did eventually run out. The final bill was for £20,000. With God in command and much help from our friends, the final payment was made a year later. My mother could never have stood the upheaval of those four months and the timing of her departure had proved right.

Chapter 24
Epilogue

The members of my family are growing up fast and I can see a time when they will need employment. It is their right to have employment if that is what they want, but work for people with handicaps is hard to find. I can for see and would hope that each would have something to do in the community, but I know that it will be difficult to find even part-time occupations for all of them.

Three years ago, with the idea of filling the gap, I decided to set up a working area to see what we could produce at home, should the need arise. It started slowly but has made steady progress. Finding sources for supplies took much time. Daring to ask other people where they got their things helped, and being bold enough to buy in large quantities, making the finished articles cheap enough to sell.

We have attempted many things. Some have been abandoned as unsuitable because they needed too much staff supervision. Others have been successful, proved interesting and have sold well.

Eleanor, one of my staff, has been very interested in this work and it is through her patience that so much has been achieved. When we make things it is necessary to market them and although a vast profit is not needed, we must cover our costs and make a little extra to continue to develop new ideas, and I have plenty of those!

Several of the girls can now sew a straight seam, using hand sewing machines which have been kindly donated. They can produce very pretty lavender bags out of donated material, ribbons and lavender. We started making re-cycled birthday cards on coloured paper. We have now progressed to a better quality card in three different sizes. Little baskets of soap also prove popular, both to make and to sell.

I am sure we could do more on the horticultural side, and with its produce, if we had a better working area; it is only lack of finance that prevents it.

The hope that started all this is still being fulfilled. Thanks to you all for what you have given me.

The proceeds from this book will go to the charity *Friends of Lynton House*
Reg Charity Nº 1000276